THE BOOK OF NEW YORK FIRSTS

THE BOOK OF NEW YORK FIRSTS

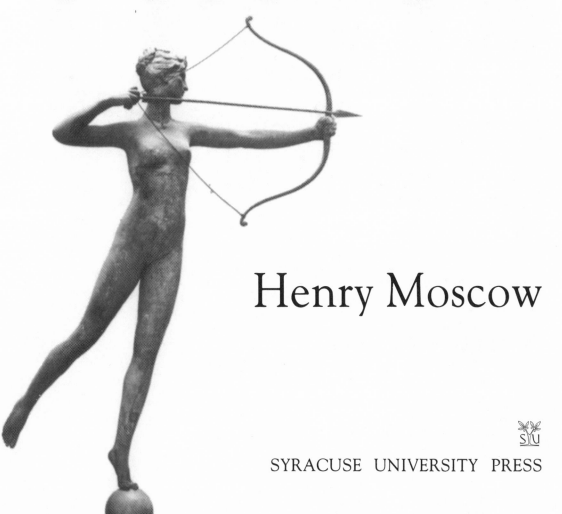

Henry Moscow

SYRACUSE UNIVERSITY PRESS

Henry Moscow worked as a submarine cable telegrapher, night editor of the *New York Telegram*, managing editor of the *New York Post*, and the editor of *Life's* international editions—a position he held for over twenty-five years. His book credits include *The Street Book*, *Thomas Jefferson and His World*, *Russia Under the Czars*, and (as coauthor) *Educational Psychology: An Introduction*.

First Syracuse University Press Edition 1995
95 96 97 98 99 00   6 5 4 3 2

The paper used in this publication meets the minimum requirements of American National Standard for Information Sciences—Permanence of Paper for Printed Library Materials, ANSI Z39.48-1984. ∞™

First published by Macmillan Publishing Co. in 1982.

Originally designed and prepared for publication by The Glusker Group, Inc. Picture research by Research Reports.

Library of Congress Cataloging-in-Publication Data
Moscow, Henry.
    The book of New York firsts / Henry Moscow.
        p.   cm.
    Originally published: New York : Collier, 1982.
    Includes index.
    ISBN 0-8156-0308-8
    1. New York (N.Y.)—History—Miscellanea.   I. Title.
F128.3.M89   1995
974.7'1—dc20   94-39250

Manufactured in the United States of America

This book is published with the assistance of a grant from the John Ben Snow Foundation.

Contents

Introduction

A few years ago, a foreign-born photographer friend of mine was lured from the New York that he loved to a small midwestern city: the enticements were a highly paid executive post in the public relations department of a great industrial company and an opportunity to spend time with his family instead of flitting to far places, on an hour's notice, lugging an arsenal of cameras. About a year after his migration from the metropolis, he returned for a visit.

"How do you like it out there, Felipe?" I asked.

"It's great," he said. "We live in a big old Victorian house with a porch that runs three quarters of the way around it, and the lawn has tremendous maples. I walk to work and I walk home for lunch. My kids walk to school, which is two blocks from the house. It's clean and quiet and living is less expensive and as far as I can tell there's practically no crime."

"Sounds good," I said, "but do you *really* like it?"

He grimaced and replied: "It's pastrami on white."

The savors that distinguish New York from other cities, great or small, have been developing since the first settlers landed in 1624. In her 19th century *History of the City of New York,* Mrs. Van Rensselaer wrote:

"Governor Stuyvesant's New Amsterdam is . . . often painted . . . as the counterpart of some insignificant seaport in the peaceful, prosperous, unexcitable Holland of today. It is described as a sleepy, slothful village of apathetic boors and burghers stupified by beer and tobacco and living in a stagnant isolation from which they were fortunately aroused by the advent of the English as their rulers.

"A seaport planted anywhere in the world by Dutchmen of the seventeenth century could not be a drowsy place, and the one that they planted on Manhattan was not an isolated place. It lived by traffic with the ever-dangerous people of the forest, with Englishmen up and down the coast, and with men of many nations eastward and southward across the sea; and it was a thoroughfare in a sense that was true of no other place on the American mainland, for those who voyaged between New England and Virginia preferred to pass through the safe waters of Long Island Sound, ships from England bound for New England often tarried in the harbor, and so at times did Dutch, French and English privateers. Life was more varied and more agitated within the 'walls and gates' that enclosed New Amsterdam's heterogeneous population, excited by many controversies and threatened by many perils, than it was in any English-American community. Rarely indeed, except in the depths of winter, can New Amsterdam have known a quiet day, never a dull, monotonous season. Liveliness was one of the few things it never lacked, torpidity one of the moods of mind it could not encourage, peaceful sloth one of the careers for which it offered no chance." In those aspects, the city has not changed.

In *The Street Book,* an earlier publication to which this is a companion, I endeavored to create a mosaic of New York's past by matching the names of Manhattan streets with the individuals who had borne those names. That format could not encompass the whole story. Neither can this little book: as its subtitle indicates, it is a potpourri of incidents and people, mostly forgotten, that over the centuries have made New York a place that never has known "a dull, monotonous season," or consumed its pastrami between slices of the not-quite-right kind of bread. Those fragments of history engross me, and I hope that they will inform and interest you.

HENRY MOSCOW

SETTLERS

New York's First White Settlers—the Belgians

If you stroll in Battery Park, where Manhattan begins and New York began, you may chance upon a modest monument close by the newly counterfeited Castle Clinton. The monument's legend, its gilded capital letters graven in the granite, delivers a deceptively discreet message that, if you *know* that New York was first settled by the Dutch, is likely to provoke a surprised "Huh?" The legend reads:

PRESENTED TO THE CITY OF NEW YORK
BY THE CONSEIL PROVINCIAL DU
HAINAUT IN MEMORY OF THE WALLOON
SETTLERS WHO CAME TO AMERICA IN
THE NIEU NEDERLAND UNDER THE
INSPIRATION OF JESSE DE FOREST OF
AVESNE, THEN COUNTY OF HAINAUT
ONE OF THE 17 PROVINCES

The monument's base is inscribed: 1624-1924

The *Nieuw Nederland* was the 260-ton Dutch ship that in 1624 brought the first of the millions of non-Indian people who live in New York. But Walloons, not Dutchmen? Walloons, of course, are French-speaking Belgians; their very name, "Walloon," derives from that of the Gauls, of whom Julius Caesar wrote: "The most formidable of these are the Belgians." Hainaut? It is a Belgian province that was part of the ancient County of Hainaut, now divided between Belgium and France. Avesne? A French town a score of miles from the present Belgian border. Jesse de Forest? Unless there were De Forests among your ancestors, you probably have never heard of him.

The names add color and detail that do not fit the conventional picture that most of us, I suspect, envision as portraying New York's beginnings. That picture looks a good deal like this: A vaguely imagined figure named Peter Minuit steps ashore from a Dutch ship sometime in 1626 carrying a trunkful of trinkets, summons together a few Indians who have never seen a white man and tricks them into selling him Manhattan Island, where a prim Dutch village soon springs up.

The truth is different. Though the admirable Dutch did indeed found New York by means of the enterprising corporation called the Dutch West India Company, the future city's first European inhabitants were largely and perhaps entirely French-speaking Belgians. When they boarded the *Nieuw*

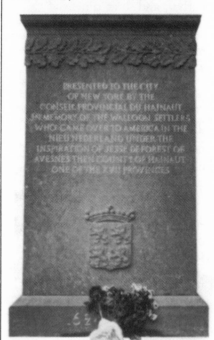

Battery Park monument to New York's first settlers was erected in 1924, the city's 300th birthday.

Penny postage stamp, issued in 1924 to mark the city's tercentennial, depicts the Nieuw Nederland, *which brought the earliest pioneers. The stamp's legend refers to Huguenots as well as Walloons, but Huguenots probably were later arrivals.*

Nederland, Captain Cornelis Jacobsen May commanding, they numbered about 110 (the figure is imprecise because in 1821 the practical Dutch sold the *Nieuw Nederland*'s passenger list and many other Dutch West India Company documents for recycling). The emigrants sailed from Holland in March, 1624—probably on the thirtieth, the day on which they formally swore to obey the Dutch West India Company's instructions. (Those instructions included a clause that Dutch was to be the official language in the colonies the emigrants were to establish.) At the voyage's start, there were thirty families; when they arrived here in May, there were thirty-four families, for the vessel had traveled via the warm waters of Madeira, the Canary Islands and the West Indies, and romance had flourished. Otherwise, the voyage was apparently uneventful almost to its end. Just outside the harbor, the *Nieuw Nederland* encountered a French vessel that had come to claim the territory for the King of France. But a Dutch ship, *De Makereel* (the Mackerel), warned off the Frenchman.

Captain May assigned eight

single young men to remain on Manhattan, sent one small party to the site of Hartford and another to the shores of the Delaware River, and re-embarked the remainder for a trip up the Hudson to settle in what is now Albany. They were not venturing into unknown territory; for at least a dozen years Dutch mariners and fur traders, including Captain May, had been coming and going—dealing with the Indians and returning, as soon as business permitted, to their *vrouwen* and the amenities of Amsterdam, the most important city of one of the world's most important powers.

Soon, letters reached home from these first settlers describing the richness of the soil, the height of the corn, the plenitude of fish and game, the immensity of the trees. The news impelled another party of Walloons—how many is unrecorded—to set out for New Netherland in January, 1625, in the ship *Oranjeboom* (Orange Tree). Arriving in late March or early April after a voyage on which eleven passengers died and twenty became ill while waiting out the weather in the harbor of plague-stricken Plymouth, England, some of the newcomers joined the eight bachelors on Manhattan. The little settlement at the island's southern tip was further reinforced, within a couple of months, with the arrival of six families and a number of unattached young folk—comprising forty-five people in all—in the ships *Paert* (Horse), *Koe* (Cow) and *Schaep* (Sheep). The national origins of the third group of immigrants are unknown; the party may have included Dutchmen as well as Walloons. Aptly named, the three ships also carried livestock, quartered in high style (see page 13). But *De Makereel*, which

had started out with them, had been captured by corsairs off Dunkirk, on April 27, two days after setting sail.

Under the supervision of one Willem ver Hulst, who had arrived in the *Oranjeboom* and had been directed by the West India Company to take charge, the settlers began busily to carry out the company's carefully detailed instructions for building a town. But the colonists shipped Ver Hulst back to Amsterdam for misconduct—what he had done we do not know—and chose Peter Minuit (see page 44) to govern them in his stead. Minuit, who was probably himself a Walloon, called in the settlers from the outposts, and by 1626 Fort Amsterdam, as the settlement was dubbed, boasted a population of two hundred, mostly Walloons.

But why Walloons when the West India Company was Dutch? Religion, economics, territorial claims, capitalist enterprise, and the ideas and energies of two men—both Walloons—contribute

to the answer. The seventeen Provinces mentioned in the Battery Park monument's legend constituted the Low Countries, which encompassed considerably more land than modern Belgium and the Netherlands. The entire region had been ruled by Catholic Spain, but the Dutch-inhabited, Protestant northern provinces had broken free and by the late 1500s Protestant Belgians—the Walloons—were moving north so that they could worship without fear and in their own language. They came mostly from Lille, Valenciennes, and Avesne, or Avesnes— all now French—in the Counties of Hainaut and Flanders, and they concentrated in the southern Dutch city of Leyden, an ancient Roman town that already boasted a great university. Two dynamic men were eventually to move them on to America. One was

Houses in background, shown in artist's concept of the landing of the Walloons, indicate this party of immigrants was not the first.

Leyden University, founded in 1575 by William of Nassau, was a familiar sight to New York's first inhabitants, who originally had taken refuge in Leyden. Drawing of the university dates to 1614.

Willem Usselinx, from Antwerp; as early as 1600, he was urging that colonies be established in such distant places as Africa and the West Indies—the term "West Indies" then embracing all of North and South America. On April 15, 1622, he persuaded the Dutch States-General and States-Provincial to appoint a commission to organize a Dutch West India Company. Jesse de Forest, a latecomer to Leyden—he settled there between 1608 and 1615, when he was in his thirties—had similar thoughts. A dyer by trade and the father of ten children, he dreamed of a richer life—an ambition understandable enough in view of the fact that in 1618 he had had to appear in court at The Hague to defend himself in a suit for the equivalent of $20. So Jesse rounded up 56 fellow-Walloons, the heads of families that totaled some 227 people, to sign a petition, in French, which he presented to England's ambassador to The Hague on July 19, 1621. They had no complaints against Dutch hospitality, but, mostly blue-collar folk, they thought they might do better economically in Virginia. (Their petition survives, by the way, in the Public Records Office in London.) The British were willing enough but they wanted to disperse the colonists in scattered settlements, and Jesse wanted to keep them together. The deal was hanging fire when Jesse got word of Usselinx's success; he immediately offered himself and his fellow-petitioners for service to the West India Company. The next day—one week after the company's agreement with Usselinx—De Forest got a favorable reply in principle; the Dutch did business fast.

Not all the petition signers were aboard the *Nieuw Nederland* when it sailed in March, 1624; some had good reason to wait. And, because of the destruction of the passenger list, the names of most of those aboard cannot be determined. It is certain, though, that among the passengers were Bastien Janszen Krol and his family, who may or may not have been typical of the settlers. Krol was an

Walls of Fort Amsterdam, at what is now Battery Park, were erected in the settlement's earliest years and the church (left of flagpole) stood within them. In this painting by Edward L. Henry, Indians (left and right foreground) arrive by boat for trading, shopping and sightseeing.

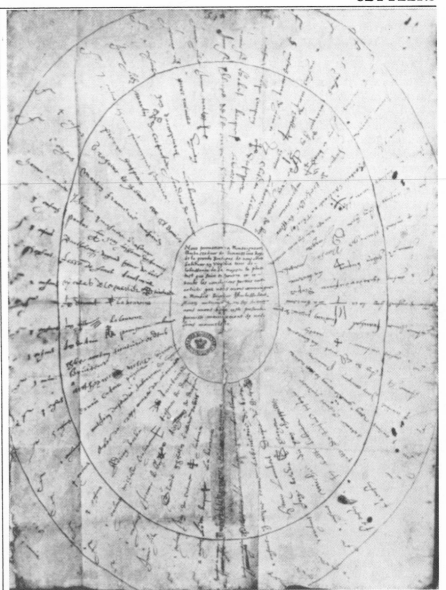

illiterate silk worker when he married in 1615, at the age of twenty, but his bride, Chrystoval, taught him to read and write. He learned so well that on November 20, 1623, he passed an examination in Amsterdam for *krankenbezoeker* ("visitor of the sick"), a lay reader qualified to conduct religious services. Within months of his arrival on Manhattan, he hurried back to Holland to ask that some-

Willem Usselinx

one be sent to baptize the babies who were one of the island's most abundant crops and to perform the marriages that preceded—or followed—parenthood. He was given permission to conduct the rites himself, and later he served briefly as director-general, or governor, of New Netherland. [He lost the job to Wouter Van Twiller, who had more influence in Amsterdam.]

Not aboard the *Nieuw Nederland* on its historic voyage was Jesse de Forest. He had gone to Guyana to set up another Dutch West India Company colony of Walloons, and he died of sunstroke on the bank of the Oyapok River, on October 22, 1624. But other De Forests were to come and to distinguish the name in the land that Jesse never saw.

There is an irony in the tale. Unlike most of the colonies on the Eastern Seaboard, the place that became New York was settled not by seekers of religious freedom—the Walloons already had it in Holland—but of economic betterment. From its birth, New York has been business-bent. Yet, along with prosperity, the settlers rejoiced in the liberty to believe and worship as they wished—a privilege denied in colonies founded chiefly for reasons of faith.

Round-robin petition of would-be settlers in America accompanied Jesse de Forest's letter to the Virginia Company suggesting a deal. But the British company's terms proved unacceptable and many of the petition's signers went instead to what became New York. The original petition, measuring 18x13½ inches, survives in London.

The First Black Settlers— Slaves Who Won Freedom

The city's first black settlers, about a dozen Angolan men, arrived as slaves in 1625 and 1626, shortly after the first whites. Since the Dutch did not engage, at least officially, in the slave trade, the blacks probably had been taken from Portuguese ships bound for Brazil from Angola, which, like Brazil, was a Portuguese colony. Fort Amsterdam, as New York was then called, must have been the Dutch port closest to the scenes of capture.

As "property" of the Dutch West India Company, the black newcomers worked the fields of wheat, rye, barley, oats, buckwheat, canary seed, and flax, loaded the company's ships with thousands of pelts of beaver, otter, mink, wildcat, and rat, and helped to build Fort Amsterdam. But eventually they were freed and given land of their own— some of it in what later became Greenwich Village, which for the following two centuries was home to much of Manhattan's black population.

The first dozen were joined in 1628 by three Angolan women slaves who quickly found husbands, and in the next few years by many free blacks who were very welcome in the labor-short town. Some of the free men, though, apparently had trouble collecting their wages; the minutes for a meeting of Dutch West India Company directors in 1634 in Amsterdam contain a note: "There was read a petition from five Negroes arrived from New Netherland, claiming to have earned eight guilders [about $2.40] a month, requesting settlement." They were referred back to New Netherland.

Ten years later, the slaves too had a petition, and it resulted in America's first emancipation proclamation, enacted on February 25, 1644. It read:

"We, [Director General] Willem Kieft and Council of New Netherland, having considered the petition of the Negroes named Paulo Angola, Big Manuel, Little Manuel, Manuel de Gerrit de Reus, Simon Congo, Anthony Portugis, Gracia, Peter Santomee, Jan Francisco, Little Anthony, Jan Fort Orange, who have served the company 18 @ 19 years, to be liberated from their servitude and set at liberty, especially as they have been many years in the service of the Hon[ble] West India Company here, and have been long since promised their freedom; also, that they are burdened with many children, so that it is impossible for them to support their

Although the city's first slaves were emancipated in 1644, slavery long persisted, and the slave market (center), shown here in 1730, was a busy place. The site was the foot of Wall Street.

wives and children, as they have been accustomed to do, if they must continue in the Company's service;

"Therefore, We, the director and Council do release, for the term of their natural lives, the above named and their Wives from Slavery, hereby setting them free and at liberty, on the same footing as other Free people here in New Netherland, where they shall be able to earn their livelihood by Agriculture on the land shewn and granted to them. . . ."

Paulo Angola was given a farm between what became Minetta Lane and Thompson Street, close to where Domingo Anthony, a free black, already lived. (The path along Minetta Brook was later called Negro Causeway.) Big Manuel's grant covered much of what is now Washington Square Park. Blacks who had never been enslaved received land along a wagon road west from the Bowery, between what became Canal Street and Astor Place, and

Minetta Lane in Greenwich Village, shown as it appears today, was the home of the first freed blacks.

The First Animal Colonists— They Traveled First Class

The first animal colonists—a hundred stallions, mares, bulls, cows, sheep, and hogs—which arrived in the summer of 1625 in the convoy made up of the *Paert*, the *Koe*, and the *Schaep*, crossed the Atlantic in relative luxury. Pieter Evertsen Hulst, an Amsterdam brewer, paid their way and boasted that "each animal has its own stall, with a floor of three feet of sand, arranged as comfortably as any stall here [in Holland]. Each animal has its respective servant who attends to it and knows what he is to get if he delivers it there alive." Fresh water was pumped to the beasts from barrels stored under a neatly contrived extra deck. Actually, only two of the ships carried animals; the third was loaded with extra feed and water in case the voyage was prolonged. (Despite the precautions, three animals did die on the way.)

On their arrival, the animals were landed on Governors Island (called by the settlers Nutten—Nut—Island), to keep them from straying in Manhattan's forests. But pasture and water were scarce on Governors Island, and almost immediately the beasts were ferried to Manhattan, where twenty of them died within the next few months after eating bad grass.

The first cattle brought from Holland were of the Holstein breed like this beast drawn in 1800.

around the Fresh Water, or Collect, close by the present Foley Square.

There were a couple of catches, though, to the emancipation. Each freed black had to pay annually "thirty skepels [baskets] of Maize, or Wheat, Pease or Beans, and one Fat hog, valued at thirty guilders" or return to slavery. And their children, born or unborn, were to be slaves.

The proviso about the children outraged some distinguished local citizens. "It is contrary to the laws of every people that any one born of a free Christian mother shall be a slave and compelled to remain in servitude," they protested to the Dutch West India Company directors in Amsterdam.

Hard-liners retorted, "Then don't convert them [blacks] to Christianity." But the hard-liners seem to have lost the argument. Lucas Santomee, the son of Peter Santomee, one of the freed slaves, became the city's first black doctor. And the Reverend Johannes Megapolensis, the dominie after the emancipation, wrote that "no more than three [children of freed slaves] are in service, viz., one which [Peter] Stuyvesant has with him on the Company's bouwerie; one at the Hope House; one wench with Martin Cregier, who has reared her from a little child at his own expense."

More slaves, sad to say, soon replaced the freedmen. The ship *Tamandara* arrived in May, 1646, with blacks from Brazil who were sold for pork and peas, and in May of 1655 the first slaves direct from Africa—they came from Guinea—were landed by the ship *Witte Paert* (White Horse). The Dutch West India Company's directors in Amsterdam had authorized Jan de Sweerts and Dirck Pietersen Wittepaert to import them because it would lead "to the increase of population and the advancement of said place [New Netherland]."

The First Italian Settler— A Castaway

The first Italian settler, Pietro Cesare Alberto, came ashore in Brooklyn in May, 1635, when Captain David de Vries's ship, *Coninck David* (King David) was wrecked just outside the harbor. A crew member who had signed on in Holland, Alberto was a twenty-seven-year-old Venetian and probably the son of Andrea Alberti, Venice's secretary of the treasury. Pietro Cesare built a house and started farming in Brooklyn's Wallabout (Walloon Bay) area; in 1642 he married a Dutch girl, Judit Jans, in the Dutch Reformed Church, and fathered seven children. The Rev-

erend Everardus Bogardus, New Amsterdam's dominie at the time, Latinized Pietro Cesare's surname to Albertus, which evolved into Alburtis and Burtis.

Another early Italian settler was Mathys Capito, who in 1655 became a bookkeeper for New Netherland's government and so was, in effect, the first of his nationality to hold a civil-service job here.

Looking across Wallabout Basin and the East River (below) to Manhattan in a gouache dating to about 1838, a naval hospital stands on rising ground (right) in the old Naval Shipyard in Brooklyn. The hospital's site is at Flushing Avenue, between Ryerson Street and Grand Avenue. Wallabout today is pictured at left.

The First English Settlers— Refugees from New England

The first Anglo-Saxons allured by what was to become New York emigrated from New England, where they had failed to find the freedom for which they had left Olde England. The first of them to look south was Captain John Underhill, who in 1638 published in London a book titled *Newes from America*, which contained the earliest description in English of New Netherland. Underhill wrote: "The truth is, I want time to set forth the excellencies of the whole Countrey; but if you would know the garden of New England, then you must glance upon Hodsons River, a place exceeding all yet named, the River affords fish in abundance, as Sturgeon, Salmon and many delicate varieties of fish that naturally lyes in the River, the only place for Beaver that we have in these parts."

Provincial seal of New Netherland, used until 1664, honored the beaver, the pelt of which served as money and was "as good as gold."

Underhill obtained permission, on September 8, 1639, to join the Dutch colony but he dallied until he was excommunicated in Massachusetts for looking lustfully at Mistress Miriam Wilbore during a lecture in Boston. It was probably Mistress Wilbore's fault: she had gone to the lecture wearing "a

Ever-defiant, Anne Hutchinson stands trial in Boston in 1637 for criticizing the clergy. She was ordered banished and then excommunicated.

pair of wanton open-worked gloves, slit at the thumbs and fingers," so that she could reach more easily for her snuff.

By the time Underhill did move, the tide of immigration from the north was flowing. John Throgmorton abandoned Salem for Throgs Neck. Lady Deborah Moody (see page 21), after carefully considering her options, passed up Salem, Boston, Providence and points in Connecticut for Gravesend, near Coney Island. Anne Hutchinson, a voluble, nimble-witted but rather fierce religious dissenter who had been excommunicated from the Massachusetts Bay Colony, settled in what became the Eastchester section of the Bronx.

When Underhill did come, he found fifty or sixty compatriots already here and he led the men among them in battle in an unprovoked war that Governor Willem Kieft initiated against the Indians in 1643. It was in retaliation that the Indians massacred Anne Hutchinson and all her family except one daughter, who was taken prisoner and, legend has it, married a chief.

The First Jews—Refugees, of Course

The first recorded Jewish colonist, Jacob bar Simson, arrived from Amsterdam on August 22, 1654, in the Dutch ship *Pereboom* (Pear Tree) after a six-and-a-half week voyage, for which he paid 36 guilders (about $14) fare. On the trip, he served as guardian for several score young orphans whom the Dutch West India Company was sending as settlers. An Ashkenazi (Northern European) Jew, Bar Simson began life here as a manual laborer. Two weeks after he landed, twenty-three Sephardic Jews arrived here from Recife, in Brazil—just in time to celebrate (on September 12-13) the first Rosh Hashanah services conducted in America. The group consisted of four men, Abraham Israel de Piza, David Israel Faro, Moses Ambrosius, or Lumbrozo, and Asser Levy van Swellem (who promptly Americanized his name to Asser Levy); their wives; two single women, Judicq de Mereda and Rycke Nounes; and thirteen children. They had had a harrowing passage. In Recife, they had been members of a thriving and influential society of six hundred Jews, but when the Portuguese retook Recife from the Dutch (who had occupied it in 1624), the Portuguese commander, Francisco de Barreto, promised safe conduct to all who wanted to leave and mobilized sixteen ships to speed their going.

Off Jamaica, the ship carrying the twenty-three fell into the hands of Spanish pirates, who stripped them of most of their possessions. A French man-of-war rescued them and put them aboard a bark named *St. Charles*, *St. Catrina*, or *St. Catherine*—the record is mutilated—which took them, as they asked, to the nearest Dutch port, New Amsterdam. Here the bark's French master, Jacques de la Motthe, demanded, 2,500 guilders, triple the normal

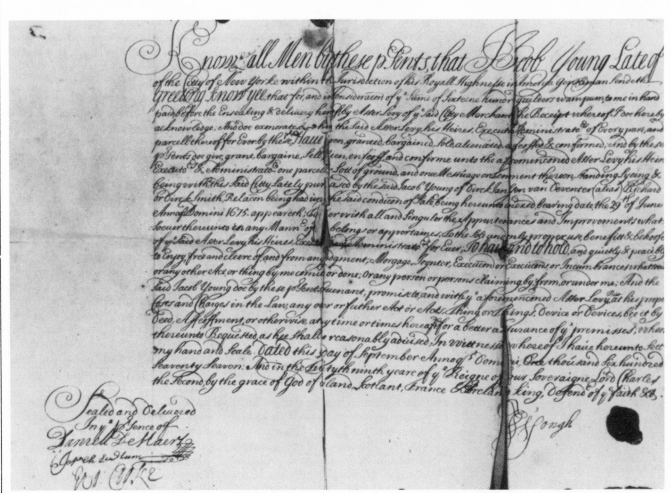

Deed executed September 5, 1677, made Asser Levy, one of the Jews who arrived in 1654, the owner of property purchased from Jacob Young.

Under Dutch rule, the Brazilian port city of Recife, pictured here about 1640, provided a lush home for some 600 Jews of Spanish and Portuguese ancestry. But they lost it when Recife changed hands.

fare. The Jews had only 933 guilders left; to collect the balance, De la Motthe attached the few goods that had escaped the pirates, and arranged an auction. The auction was set for Rosh Hashanah, but the Jews asked for a postponement on religious grounds and the court granted the delay, thus according Judaism its first legal recognition in America. At the auction, which was held the day after Rosh Hashanah, sympathetic New Amsterdamers kept the bidding low and noncompetitive, and returned the few treasures to their owners. Furious, De la Motthe stopped the sale and sued to have David Israel Faro and Moses Ambrosius jailed until they paid the 1,567-guilder debt. The Dutch court assented at a beery session, but cannily ruled that De la Motthe would have to pay for the two men's board in prison. While De la Motthe calculated the possible cost, the Jews' lawyer, Solomon Pietersen, made a discovery in the fine script of their contract with the Frenchman: 933 guilders exceeded De la Motthe's share of the passage money—the balance was due to the sailors. Pietersen persuaded the crewmen to wait until the Jews could get money from Amsterdam, and the dispute ended there.

(How Pietersen, himself a Jew, got involved in the affair remains a mystery. No record exists of his arrival, and he may have preceded even Bar Simson—in confirmation of the dictum that "no Jew is ever the first Jew to arrive anywhere, there has always been one before him.")

The Jews' troubles were not over, however. Almost immediately, Governor Peter Stuyvesant, who loathed all dissenters from his own Calvinism, attempted to expel the newcomers from the colony. On September 22, he wrote to the Dutch West India Company's directors that he "deemed it useful to require" the Jews "in a friendly way to depart" and that he hoped the "deceitful race" would not be "allowed further to infect and trouble this new colony." The directors replied that to ban Jews "would be somewhat unreasonable and unfair," especially because of heavy losses they had suffered in Brazil and "the large amount of capital which they still have invested in the shares of this company."

The First Ethnics— Into the Melting Pot

The first so-called "ethnics" arrived in wide variety on the heels of the Belgians, the blacks, and the Dutch. Less than two decades after Peter Minuit bought Manhattan, the Jesuit missionary Father (now Saint) Isaac Jogues, who visited here in 1643, reported: "On the island of Manhate, and in its environs, the Director General [Willem Kieft] told me that there were men of eighteen different languages." Among those whom Father Jogues encountered were an Irish Catholic who had married a Protestant Walloon widow, the shy Portuguese Catholic bride of a non-Catholic Dutch army officer, and a young Polish Lutheran bachelor.

Relatively late in arriving, these immigrants of 1656 get a first look at a fast-growing town.

The First Chinese—
Straight to Mott Street

The first recorded Chinese immigrant in New York was Ah Ken, a Cantonese who arrived in 1858 and opened a cigar store on Park Row. He lived on Mott Street. He was joined in 1866 or 1867 by Wah Kee, another Cantonese, who came east from San Francisco; Wah Kee set up shop at 13 Pell Street, selling vegetables, preserved fruits, and curios. By 1880, Chinese were settling here in large numbers.

By 1909, when this photograph of Doyers Street was snapped, Chinatown had become a bustling community whose residents and merchants proudly flew the flag of their adopted country on national holidays.

The First Germans—
Under British Auspices

It is not known who the first German to come to New York was, but in the summer of 1710 some three thousand Germans arrived. They came from the Palatinate, whence they had been driven by Louis XIV of France. The British Parliament granted them £10,000 sterling to pay their way here and establish themselves as manufacturers of tar for the Royal Navy. Many stayed in New York, where they built a church on the site of Grace Church, at Broadway and 10th Street; some moved to Livingston Manor in the Catskills; but the majority settled in Pennsylvania, where they became the "Pennsylvania Dutch." Among those who stayed in New York was a ten-year-old boy named John Peter Zenger, who became an apprentice to the city's first printer, William Bradford, and who, as a newspaper editor and publisher, helped establish the principle of freedom of the press.

Andrew Hamilton, a famous lawyer of the time, defends Zenger at trial involving freedom of the press.

EXTRAORDINARY PEOPLE

The Versatile Doctor

The city's first physician, Jean Mousnier de la Montagne, arrived in the spring of 1637 after years of planning to go to America; he had been an associate of Jesse de Forest, who inspired the first settlers (see page 8), and was with De Forest when De Forest died in the Guyana jungle in 1624. A member of a French family long distinguished in literature, theology, and medicine, La Montagne matriculated at the University of Leyden's medical school in 1619, at the age of twenty-four, but he interrupted his studies repeatedly for such ventures as exploring Guyana before he began practicing at Leyden. La Montagne landed here with his wife, Rachel—the daughter of the Walloon landlady of his student days—and four small children, one of whom, a girl, had been born at sea on the way. He quickly established himself as a leading citizen: Governor Willem Kieft appointed him to the colony's council; his signature appears frequently on the colony's laws; and he became one of the founders of Harlem. After the British took New Amsterdam, La Montagne disappeared from history; he probably returned to Holland with his friend Peter Stuyvesant to explain why the city had been yielded without a fight, and died while abroad. A daughter married Jacob Kip, of the family for whom Kips Bay is named; they lived on an estate at what is now 35th Street and Park Avenue.

More than a century after La Montagne helped to found Harlem, the settlement retained a rural character. This view "across the upper Harlem valley, looking to the north" dates to about 1770.

The Unpaid Surgeon

The first surgeon to practice in the city was Harmen Myndertsen van de Bogaert, who arrived in the ship *Endracht* on May 24, 1630, and like many of his successors, had trouble collecting unpaid bills. Ten years after his arrival he sued the Dutch West India Company for compensation for his services from March 21, 1630—the day he sailed from the Netherlands—to February 1, 1633. Whether or not he won is unrecorded. He died in 1648. His successors, it seems, did not enjoy booming practices, for they petitioned Governor Peter Stuyvesant and the New Netherland Council on February 12, 1652, for the exclusive right to shave as barbers. They got the reply that "shaving is properly not in the province of the surgeons, but is only an appendix to their calling, that nobody can be prevented to please himself in this matter or to serve anybody else for friendship's sake, out of courtesy and without receiving payment for it." But "keeping a shop to do it in" was "expressly forbidden," and, apparently in the interest of fairness, ships' barbers were forbidden to "dress any wounds, bleed or prescribe for any one on land" without consent of the surgeons, or "at least Dr. La Montagne."

The Quarrelsome Teacher

The city's first schoolteacher—and the first headmaster of what is now the Collegiate School (see page 89)—was Adam Roelantsen, a thirty-two-year-old Frieslander who arrived in the ship *Harinck* (Herring) on March 28, 1638, in the company of Director General Willem Kieft. Roelantsen, who had been here before, in 1633, quickly proved to be the most quarrelsome and litigious man in town. By June 9, 1638, he had been made defendant in a suit to recover an estate, and the same year he sued and was sued for slander. The next year had barely begun when, in January, he was involved in another slander suit—in August of 1640 he became party to still another; then in September he sued Gillis de Voocht for wages for laundry work. (Roelantsen washed dirty linen outside of court as well as in.) He lost the De Voocht case because the money was not yet due him.

It could not have been the strain of teaching that made Roelantsen so disputatious, because even after he became the Dutch West India Company's weighmaster in 1643 and a jailer in 1647, he continued to get in trouble. In 1646, he signed over to Govert Aertsen the house that Roelantsen had built on Stone Street, between Whitehall and Broad streets, next to Philip Geraerdy's tavern (see page 38); he made the deal just in time to keep the house out of the hands of the law. Eleven days later, he was tried and convicted of grossly insulting a neighbor's wife. He was sentenced to be publicly whipped and then banished from the colony. But his wife had just died while he was on a trip to Holland, and he had four chil-

dren, so the court delayed execution of the sentence, and apparently it was never carried out. At the same time he had other problems: on arriving back here from Holland, he removed some articles from his luggage before it had been inspected, and the ensuing row resulted in a suit for slander by the inspector; he was sued also for the passage money for himself and the son who accompanied him, but he beat that case by claiming that they had worked their way over. And the next year, 1647, he sued Jan Teunissen, the carpenter who had built his house, for an alleged debt. Roelantsen last appears in the records in 1653, when he was a soldier in the militia and a woodcutter; his final court case involved his charge that Stoeffel Elsers had called him from his work in the church and beaten him up. Elsers denied it—and the quarrelsome teacher disappeared from history.

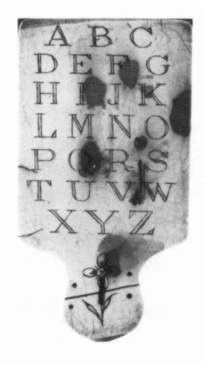

The Lawyer Who Could Not Plead

The city's only lawyer in 1653, Adriaen van der Donck, was denied permission to practice in court despite his good credentials. The directors of the Dutch West India Company in Amsterdam had written to Governor Peter Stuyvesant that "Van der Donck has been granted the right to practice as an advocate, he having received his degree at law from the University of Leyden and been admitted to the bar by the Court of Holland." But Van der Donck was restricted here to advising clients; he was barred from pleading cases on the sensible enough ground that there was no other lawyer to present opposing arguments. His exclusion from court lasted through 1654, after which he had competition. In the interim, he could not have lacked for cash: he had a grant of land, extending from the Hudson to the Sawmill River, that embraced the site of Yonkers, which he founded. The river gets its name from the sawmill he built, and Yonkers from what was known as De Jonkheer's ("the young lord's") land. In his spare time, Van der Donck wrote a history of New Amsterdam, the first ever compiled.

An early non-electronic aid to teaching, the hornbook helped children to learn the alphabet in such schools as Roelantsen's. It derives its name from the animal horn that framed elaborate models.

The Liberated Lady

The city's first liberated woman came to town in 1643. She was Lady Deborah Moody (nee Dunch), daughter of a Member of Parliament who descended from the Earl of Lincoln and was kin to Oliver Cromwell. Left a widow with a son and daughter after ten years of marriage to Henry Moody—who had been knighted and then made a baronet—she became bored with her Wiltshire home, got the required permission to visit London, overstayed her leave, and was ordered back to the provinces by the authorities. [By law, landowners could not stay away long from their property, to become absentee landlords.] So she packed up and in 1640 departed for New England's Salem, in quest of freedom. But Salem's rigid politics, infant baptism, and witch-burning aroused her passionate disapproval, which Salem reciprocated by excommunicating her. When Roger Williams, exiled from Massachusetts, did not encourage her to join him in Rhode Island, she bought a boat, loaded it in Boston with Puritan Anabaptists—whose faith she herself rejected—and sailed it around Cape Cod. She looked in on Providence and quickly decided to pass it up. She moved on to New Haven, another center of dissent, disagreed with the leadership there, and headed for New Netherland. Governor Willem Kieft, who had enough trouble on his hands with an Indian War, listened to her and took her out to the neighborhood of Coney Island, about as far from New Amsterdam as he could go in a busy week. But he granted her a land patent—the first ever given to a woman—which she shared with her son, Sir Henry, and George Baxter and James Hub-

Lady Moody (with staff) explores the site of her planned community. The legend on this mural, which used to adorn a Brooklyn bank, reads: "Lady Deborah Moody, Sir Henry her son and Governor Kieft of New Amsterdam, Ensign Geo. Baxter, Sgt. J. Hubbard and others visit the land assigned to them to consider a general pattern for a town to be called Gravesend." Kieft was doing the assigning.

bard; this patent provided for absolute freedom of conscience and the settlers' right to choose their own form of government.

Lady Moody laid out a town, which she called Gravesend, after the Moodys' place of origin in England; she got farms going and prospering, established a school, and built a church for the Anabaptists with whom she differed. Though not a Quaker, she welcomed a Quaker meeting—the first in the New World—to the house she erected. She devised a government that combined elements of the New England town meeting with local Dutch practice, and when Peter Stuyvesant succeeded Willem Kieft as governor, he used to go to her house to chat and to help settle arguments among the villagers. When not occupied by the problems of Gravesend, Lady Moody read Latin, browsed in her library, which was the biggest in New Netherland, and kept in touch with nonconformist political and religious movements. She lived in Gravesend until her death in 1659; a house said to have been hers survives, much altered, on Gravesend Neck Road between Van Sicklen Street and Mac-Donald Avenue in Brooklyn.

House identified as that of Lady Moody stands at 27 Neck Road, in Gravesend, now part of Brooklyn.

Jacques Cortelyou's Castello Plan of the city in 1660 reflects Manhattan's rapid growth, with houses solidly banked between farms and orchards. The reproduction here is of a redraft prepared in 1916 by John Wolcott Adams.

The First Commuter

The city's—and America's—first commuter began his round trips in 1656. He was Jacques Cortelyou, who had a Long Island house on a bluff overlooking the Narrows and a rented engineering office in Manhattan's Marketfield, of which Marketfield Street, near Bowling Green, is a remnant. Apart from his garb, conventional for his time, Cortelyou would have been difficult to distinguish from his modern professional counterparts: college-trained, he was outspoken, skeptical of bureaucracy, and quick to seize opportunity—as he demonstrated when he chose to come to America in 1652 at the age of twenty-seven. Cornelis van Werckhoven, a city father of Cortelyou's native Utrecht, in the Netherlands, planned a couple of real-estate developments here and wanted to look the places over before he risked any guilders; he invited Cortelyou to accompany him because Cortelyou knew Latin, spoke French in addition to Dutch, had studied philosophy and mathematics at the University of Utrecht, and would make an ideal tutor for Van Werckhoven's two young sons. Shortly after their arrival, New Amsterdam's first government (as distinct from New Netherland's) was established on February 2, 1653, and the new city fathers immediately offered Cortelyou one of the town's most important jobs. It was that of *schout*, which combined the duties of sheriff, prosecutor, and president of magistrates. Cortelyou examined the instructions that accompanied the appointment and rejected the post on the ground that the instructions were too inhibiting. He had enough to do anyway, working for Van Werckhoven and helping him lay out a village in what is now Brooklyn. When Van Werckhoven returned to the Netherlands, in 1654, he left Cortelyou behind to act as his agent; Van Werckhoven died the following year and Cortelyou became the village's true father, naming it New Utrecht in honor of his birthplace. Officialdom continued to keep a wishful eye on him, though, and on January 23, 1657, he was appointed surveyor general of New Netherland. (It was characteristic of the city that nobody minded that Cortelyou was "not a good Christian" but a Cartesian, "regulating himself and all externals by reason and justice only.") From his Marketfield office, to which he traveled regularly from Long Island, Cortelyou mapped the nascent metropolis; within the office, his draughtsmen completed the so-called Castello Plan of 1660-1662, a copy of which hangs on a wall in the New York Public Library. (The plan, a map of New Amsterdam, gets its name from the fact that the original was discovered, curiously, in an Italian palazzo in the twentieth century.) And like many a modern commuter, Cortelyou had to make lengthy business trips; his assignments outside the city included the mapping of Schenectady.

Cortelyou died in 1693, after having refused for more than twenty years to swear allegiance to the British Crown. (The British acquired New Netherland in 1664; Cortelyou finally took the oath in 1687.) He left half a dozen sons and two daughters, and his descendants have long been multifarious in the metropolitan area; Cortelyou Road in Flatbush honors the family's name. Unfortunately, nobody knows how the first commuter traveled.

The Pioneer Printer

The city's first printer, William Bradford, who set up shop at 81 Pearl Street in 1693, had more claims to distinction that the fact that he established New York's first newspaper, the *New York Gazette*, and started Manhattan's great book-publishing industry. An English-born Quaker, he was involved in America's first free-

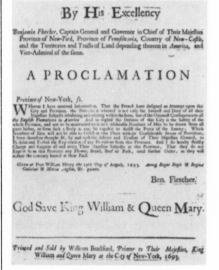

By His Excellency

Benjamin Fletcher, Captain General and Governor in Chief of Their Majesties Province of New-York, Province of Pensilvania, Country of New-Castle, and the Territories and Tracts of Land depending thereon in America, and Vice-Admiral of the same.

A PROCLAMATION

Province of New-York, ss.

WHEREAS I have received Information, That the French have designed an Attempt upon this City and Province, the Prevention whereof is not only the Interest and Duty of all their Majesties Subjects inhabiting and residing within the same, but of the Utmost Consequence to all the English Plantations in America: And to inglish the Defence of this Colony for the Safety of the whole Province, and not to be maintained without considerable Numbers of Men to be drawn from all parts hither, in time such a Body as may be capable to Repell the Force of the Enemy...

Given at Fort William Henry the 19th Day of August, 1693. Anno Regni Regis & Reginæ Gulielmi & Mariæ Angliæ, &c. quinto.

Ben. Fletcher.

God Save King William & Queen Mary.

Printed and Sold by William Bradford, Printer to Their Majesties, King William and Queen Mary at the City of New-York, 1693.

Dated 1693, the year Bradford set up shop in New York, the proclamation represents one of his earliest jobs for the provincial government.

dom-of-the-press case; tried in Philadelphia on a charge of having printed a seditious pamphlet, he argued that a printer had the obligation to print whatever a citizen wanted to say. The trial ended inconclusively because a witness dropped the evidence—a printer's form—and pied the type, so Bradford went free. He came to New York at the invitation of the governor. Here he turned down a young job-seeking Bostonian and suggested that the youth try Philadelphia; the applicant was Benjamin Franklin. Among the

When Bradford opened his Pearl Street printing establishment, Pearl Street was on the East River waterfront. Boats beached below the rutted road and the Watergate (background) stood at the street's far end. The house (left) was Captain Kidd's.

apprentices whom Bradford did hire was a young German named John Peter Zenger, who later founded a newspaper of his own and helped make freedom of the press sacrosanct in America.

Bradford's first job in New York was to print the laws and acts of the General Assembly; in his first year, he received thirty-eight government contracts. (Responding to complaints about typographical errors, Bradford set the pitch for his many successors' excuses by pointing to the rush of orders and the scarcity of good proofreaders.) Expanding into book publishing, Bradford chose for his first venture *A Paraphrastical Exposition*, by John Philly. How that one sold is not recorded, but other books kept pouring off Bradford's presses, including, in 1696, a volume called *A Letter of Advice to a Young Gentleman Leaving the University, Concerning His Behavior and Conversation in the World*, by R. L. (For a how-to book, it appeared in an unlikely market—New York had no university at the time.)

But Bradford remained successful until his death, at the age of eighty-nine, in 1752, and was buried in Trinity churchyard. Fittingly, there is a typo on his tombstone: the year of his birth is given as 1660; in fact it was 1663. Also fittingly, his tombstone went into a second edition; the original is in the New-York Historical Society. The stone now standing over Bradford's grave dates from 1863, when it was erected by the Trinity vestry because the first one had worn out.

William Bradford's tombstone in Trinity Church's yard is an 1863 replica of the original.

The Hero of the Village

The city's first social lion, and the man who made Greenwich Village fashionable, was Admiral Sir Peter Warren, for whom Warren Street is named. A bewigged, sensuous-lipped Irishman, Warren won a fortune as a captain in the British Navy: a sixteen-ship squadron he commanded, operating off Martinique, captured twenty-four French and Spanish prizes between February 12 and June 24, 1744, and one vessel alone carried £250,000 in silver. Warren landed most of the swag here, selling it through "Messieurs Stephen de Lancey & Company," who advertised it in *The Weekly Post-Boy* of June 30, 1744. Warren quickly charmed and married pretty Susannah de Lancey, daughter of the head of the De Lancey firm, and used his gains to buy three hundred acres and build a fine house in Greenwich Village. (The house survived until 1865.) No man in town cut a finer figure—especially after Warren captured Louisburg on Cape Breton Island in 1745, depriving the French of command over the gateway to the St. Lawrence. (The city rewarded him with land to add to his estate.) But Warren returned to London where he was elected to Parliament in 1747. He is buried in Westminster Abbey, and a monument there bears an epitaph written by Samuel Johnson:

Peter Warren (above) was knighted and promoted from commodore to admiral after his colonial forces captured Louisburg in an amphibious landing (below) following a forty-day siege.

Sacred to the memory
of Sir PETER WARREN,
Knight of the Bath,
Vice-Admiral of the Red Squadron
of the British Fleet,
and Member of Parliament
For the City and Liberty of Westminster.

He Derived his Descent from an Antient
Family of IRELAND;
His Fame and Honours from his Virtues
and Abilities.
How eminently these were displayed,
With what vigilance and spirit they were
exerted,
In the various services wherein he had
the
honour
To command,
And the happiness to conquer,
Will be more properly recorded in the
Annals of
GREAT BRITAIN.

On this tablet Affection with truth must
say
That, deservedly esteemed in private life,
And universally renowned for his public
conduct
The judicial and gallant Officer
Possessed all the amiable qualities of the
Friend, the Gentleman, and the Chris-
tian:
But the ALMIGHTY,
Whom alone he feared and whose
gracious protection
He had often experienced,
Was pleased to remove him from a place
of Honour,
To an eternity of happiness,
On the 29th day of July, 1752,
In the 49th year of his age.

Warren's three daughters inherited his estate here. Charlotte, the
eldest, married the Earl of
Abingdon; Abingdon Square is
named for her. Ann married
Charles Fitzroy, who became
Baron Southampton; New York
used to have a Fitzroy Road,
which paralleled Eighth Avenue
from 14th Street to 42nd Street.
Susannah married Colonel William Skinner; Christopher Street
used to be called Skinner Road.
When the estate was divided
among them, a toss of dice determined who got what. Lady
Abingdon's share was fifty-five
acres and the house, which she
sold in 1788 for $2,200. It stood
in the block bounded by Charles,
Perry, Bleecker and West Fourth
Streets.

The Maybe Heroine

The city's least remembered hero-
ine—if the tale that swept New
York early in the Revolutionary
War was true—was Phoebe
Fraunces, one of the five daugh-
ters of Samuel Fraunces of
Fraunces Tavern. Phoebe, whose

*Portrait of Washington adorns modern
sign that hangs outside Fraunces Tavern.*

father was a black West Indian
and a friend and associate of
George Washington, served as
housekeeper for Washington and
General Israel Putnam when,
early in 1776, they made their
headquarters at Richmond Hill,
the splendid house that stood at
what is now the corner of
Charlton and Varick streets. One
of Washington's bodyguards there
was Thomas Hickey, who said he
had deserted from the British
Army. That much is fact.

According to the story, Hickey
fell in love with pretty Phoebe,
and confided to her that he had
been planted by the Loyalist governor, William Tryon—who was
living on the British warship *Asia*
in the harbor—to murder Washington and as many other high
rebel officers as he could. Leading

Hickey on, Phoebe agreed to help,
and at dinner one night she
served Washington peas in which
Hickey had mixed the poison
Paris green. But as Phoebe presented the peas, she whispered a
warning. Washington tossed the
peas out the window, and
chickens in the garden, gobbling
them, soon fell dead.

Whether or not that part of the
story is fact, Washington was convinced that there was an assassi-
nation plot and he jailed the city's
Tory mayor as one of the conspir-
ators. Understandably, neither the
patriots nor the Loyalists revealed
many details. Hickey was hanged
at Grand and Chrystie streets on
June 28, 1775; his execution was
the first of a soldier in the American Army, and twenty thousand
people turned out to watch him
die. Phoebe's role remains undocumented and a 1901 suggestion
that a plaque in her honor be
affixed to Fraunces Tavern was
never adopted.

*Site of Hickey's execution as it looks
today.*

The Dauntless Woman M.D.

New York's—and America's—first woman physician was Elizabeth Blackwell, whom twenty-nine medical colleges rejected before Geneva (later Hobart) at Geneva, New York, accepted her in 1847. She did not know it, but Hobart's students—whom the administration had consulted—voted to take her as a possible source of amusement; when she showed up in a Quaker bonnet on her first day of

Elizabeth Blackwell, M.D.

school, her future colleagues pelted her with paper darts. She was graduated two years later with the best record in the class.

Born in Counterslip, Bristol, England, in 1821, Elizabeth came to America in 1832 with her family; her father, a sugar refiner, championed such causes as equal rights for women and the abolition of slavery, and helped shape her philosophy. She determined on medicine as a career when a woman friend who was dying of cancer said to her, "You are fond of study, Elizabeth. You have health, leisure and a cultivated intelligence. Why don't you devote these qualities to the service of suffering women? Why don't you study medicine? Had I been treated by a woman doctor, my worst sufferings would have been spared me."

After obtaining her M.D., Dr. Blackwell studied for several years in London and Paris, lost an eye

Women medical students busily dissect cadavers in an 1870 engraving of Dr. Blackwell's college.

in treating an infant for purulent ophthalmia, and returned to America ready to work in a clinic. But no institution would accept her, and at one place in New York she was told in jest to open her own infirmary. She did: with $150 in capital and the encouragement of the editors Horace Greeley and Charles A. Dana and a lawyer, Theodore Sedgwick, she established a dispensary at 207 East Seventh Street in Manhattan, in 1853. Her first few, initially wary women patients spread word of their satisfaction and by the year's end the dispensary was on its way to becoming what is now the New York Infirmary, a ten-story, 251-bed, nonprofit teaching hospital at Stuyvesant Square East and 15th Street. (Late in 1978, the Infirmary announced plans to merge with Beekman Downtown Hospital.) At the outbreak of the Civil War, Dr. Blackwell added to the infirmary the nation's first nursing school, to train nurses for the Union Army, and in 1864 set up the Women's Medical College. (The college thrived until Cornell began admitting women medical students in 1899.) Dr. Blackwell later helped to found the London School of Medicine for Women. She died in Hastings, England, in 1910.

The First Chiropodist

The first man to call himself a chiropodist was John Littlefield, who adopted the term to upgrade the profession of corn doctor when he opened a practice at 453 Broadway, between Grand and Howard streets, in 1844.

Though stylish, comfortable shoes like this were available, corn doctors did not lack business.

27

RELIGION

The Sermon in the Mill

The city's first religious service led by an ordained clergyman was conducted in uncertain French by a Dutch Reformed minister, Dominie Jonas Michaëlius, soon after his arrival in April, 1628. In the

Jonas Michaëlius

loft of a mill at 20-22 South William Street, Michaëlius administered the Sacrament of the Lord's Supper to fifty communicants, mostly French-speaking Walloons, and read a sermon in French "because I could not trust myself extemporaneously [in that language]." Before he arrived, the colonists had prayed in the mill loft under the guidance of *krankenbezoekers*—"visitors of the sick"—laymen with some religious training who were paid to read the Bible and keep their eyes on community morals.

The congregation got its first church in 1633. A plain, rectangular wooden structure, it stood by the East River at 33-39 Pearl Street, across from the future site of Fraunces Tavern. (Before landfill, 33-39 Pearl Street was on the waterfront.) The building was the first landmark to succumb prematurely to the city's compulsion to tear down and build bigger. In 1642, when the church was only nine years old, Captain David de Vries, an influential settler and landholder, complained to Director General (Governor) Willem Kieft that "it was a scandal to us when the English passed there and saw only a mean barn in which we preached; the first thing which the English in New England built, after their dwellings

Complete with tower and bell, St. Nicholas Church stood within the crowded walls of Fort Amsterdam.

This Dutch church, pictured here in 1731, stood in Nassau Street, between Liberty and Cedar streets, from 1729 to 1844. After 1844, the building was leased to the government for use as a post office, a function it continued to perform until 1875.

was a fine church, and we ought to do so too."

Kieft thereupon obtained 100 guilders (about $50) from De Vries as the first contribution to a building fund. The fund then encountered slow going; everyone wanted a new church but no one was prepared to pay for it. So Kieft slyly bided his time; after the fifth round of drinks at a wedding reception for the stepdaughter of the Reverend Everardus Bogardus (who had succeeded Michaëlius as dominie), Kieft announced he was accepting pledges for contributions. The now jovial burghers signed up like garment manufacturers at a UJA-Federation dinner. Next morning they had second thoughts, but Kieft would not let them off their hooks.

The new church was:
▶ the first edifice in America to be financed by an arm-twisting fund drive;
▶ the first public building in America on which a governor

contrived to advertise himself as a force for progress;

▶ the first church in America to set its congregation arguing over where to build it.

Kieft proposed a site within Fort Amsterdam, on what is now Bowling Green. A majority of the parishioners objected that the fort already was too crowded and that a tall building would shut off the power supply of nearby windmills. A few supported the fort site but demurred at giving their real rea-son—that they wanted a refuge when the Indians lost their tempers over some new Kieft-provoked outrage. (Kieft was all for having other white settlers attack Indians, and he stirred up several small but furious wars.) The minority won.

The new church, constructed of stone and heavy timber, was 70 feet long, 52 feet wide, and 16 feet high, and boasted a tower, a bell, and a peaked roof covered with oak shingles that aged to resemble slate. John and Richard Ogden of Stamford, the contractors, got 2,500 guilders (about $1,250) for the job, plus a 100-guilder bonus for good work. When it was finished, Kieft affixed a marble slab

Great fire of 1835 which ravaged lower Manhattan razed newer Dutch Reformed Church in Garden Street—now Exchange Place—and Kieft's plaque, which had been affixed to the edifice, vanished forever. View here is eastward from Garden Street, with firemen still fighting flames.

to its front. The inscription read:

Ao. Do
MDCXLII
W. Kieft Dr. Gr.
Heeft de Gemeenten
dese Tempel
doen Bouwen

[Anno Domini 1642. Willem Kieft, Director General, had the people build this temple.]

Named St. Nicholas Church, the building did provide a refuge during Indian raids; and, as foreseen, it cut off the wind from the windmills, causing flour shortages. But it survived for ninety-nine years, and when Fort Amsterdam was demolished in 1787 to make way for a mansion known as Government House, Kieft's memorial slab was found in the mud. The slab was then affixed to a new Dutch church on Garden

West End Collegiate Church on West End Avenue is one of the four that descend from the 1628 prayer meetings led by Dominie Jonas Michaëlius.

Street—now Exchange Place—where it was lost in the great fire in 1835.

Dominie Michaëlius's old congregation still flourishes, though. It was chartered as the Collegiate Reformed Dutch Church in 1696—a year before Trinity Church—by King William III of England, who was Dutch himself; it now counts 6,680 baptized members and maintains the Marble Collegiate Church at Fifth Avenue and 29th Street, the Middle Church at Second Avenue and Seventh Street, the West End Collegiate Church at West End Avenue and 77th Street, the Fort Washington Collegiate Church at Fort Washington Avenue and 181st Street, the Collegiate School on West 77th Street, and a corporation office at 45 John Street, within a short walk of the congregation's first meeting place in the mill loft on South William Street.

The Adventurous Father Jogues

The first Roman Catholic priest in the city arrived in 1643, but only as a visitor. He was the Jesuit missionary Father Isaac Jogues, who was canonized in 1930; although Catholicism was proscribed in New Amsterdam, he came as an honored guest. Having barely escaped being burned alive by Iroquois in the northern part of the colony, Father Jogues was invited to Manhattan by Director General Willem Kieft and was smuggled down the Hudson on a Dutch ship. He was accompanied by a Dutch Reformed clergyman, the Reverend Johannes Megapolensis Jr. (né

Rosh Hashanah, 1654

The first Jewish holiday services conducted anywhere in what became the United States were held here in observance of Rosh Hashanah on September 12-13, 1654, a week after the arrival of twenty-three Jews from Brazil (see page 16). New Amsterdam forbade public worship by anyone except members of the Dutch Reformed Church, but the holiday won legal recognition—the first accorded to Judaism in America—by the postponement of an auction that had been scheduled for that date. The ceremonies were held in private; the place of worship is not known, but it may have been in the loft of the mill at 20-22 South William Street, where the first settlers had prayed nearly thirty years earlier. By 1695, the twenty Jewish families here had a synagogue and a rabbi—the city's first—Saul Brown (who had anglicized his name from the Spanish Pardo). The synagogue was on the south side of Beaver Street, between Broad-

Grootstede), a former Roman Catholic, "who showed me much kindness," Father Jogues wrote. "He was supplied with a number of bottles, which he dealt out lavishly, especially on coming to an island, to which he wished that my name should be given with the noise of the cannon and of the bottles; each one manifests his love in his own fashion."

"This good father [Jogues] was received in Manate [Manhattan] with great tokens of affection," a fellow-priest, Father Buteux, reported. "The captain [Kieft] had a black coat made for him, sufficiently light, and gave him also a good cloak and a hat in their own [Dutch] style. The inhabitants came to see him, showing, by

their looks and their words, that they felt great sympathy for him. . . . A good lad, having met him in a retired place, fell at his feet, taking his hands to kiss them, and exclaiming, 'Martyr, Martyr of Jesus Christ!' He [Father Jogues] questioned him and ascertained that he was a Lutheran, whom he could not aid for want of acquaintance with his language, he was a Pole."

But Father Jogues did hear a confession, the first ever made in Manhattan. The confessant is identified in the records only as "an Irish Catholic arriving at Manate from Virginia," but it is likely that he was Hugh O'Neal, who married a Dutch widow.

Three years after his visit to New Amsterdam, Father Jogues was martyred by Mohawk Indians.

way and Broad Street, and just opposite New Street, according to a map drawn by a British military chaplain, John Miller; but Miller drew his map from memory after he had returned home. A later but more substantial source, a real-estate document dated 1700, describes a lot on the north side of Mill Street (now South William Street) as being bounded "on the east by the house and ground of John Harperding, now commonly known by the name of the Jews' synagogue." A shoemaker, Harperding—for whom John Street is named—collected £8 a year rent; then the congregation bought a lot from him at what is now 18 South William Street for £100, a loaf of sugar, and a pound of Bohea tea (black, and at the time the best grade), and erected a temple that served the congregation—Shearith Israel, or Remnant of Israel—for the first three decades of the eighteenth century.

Current, long-time home of Shearith Israel, the Spanish and Portuguese Synagogue, is on Central Park West.

Erected in 1846, present Trinity Church was designed by Richard Upjohn, who drew this picture in 1847.

The Church That Everyone Paid For

The first Trinity Church, chartered by King William III (of the team of William and Mary) on May 6, 1697, stood on the site of the present edifice but it turned its back on Broadway and Wall Street and faced the Hudson, which lapped the shore at Greenwich Street. Before it was built, members of the Church of England worshipped in the Dutch Reformed Church. Funds for building the church were raised by contributions from almost everyone in town, including nonconformist Protestants and at least half a dozen of the twenty Jewish families. The donors' names survive faintly in an ancient church ledger, with the Jews pointedly listed on a separate page.

The fund afforded only a low, unimposing structure that for years after the church's first services, on May 13, 1698, lacked a steeple. Enlarged and adorned in 1737, the building burned down in 1776 in a city-wide conflagration supposedly started by American patriots. (The fire deprived George Washington of his Manhattan house of worship.) A second Trinity, consecrated in 1790 with President Washington in attendance, had to be torn down in 1839 after it was damaged by a heavy snowfall. The present building, designed by Richard Upjohn, an English immigrant who became the first president of the American Institute of Architects, was consecrated in 1846.

A royal gift of land in 1705 eventually made Trinity one of the richest parishes in the country, but it resulted also in lawsuits and claims that plagued the congregation for more than a century. The land, which ran roughly from Broadway to the Hudson

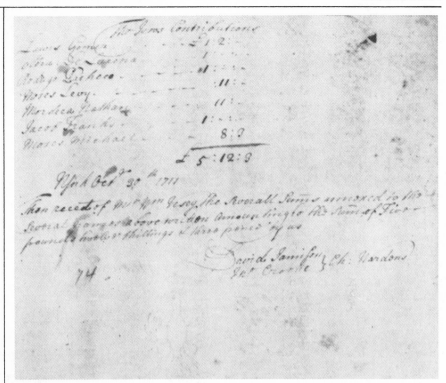

Jewish contributors to the building fund of the first Trinity Church appear on separate page of ledger.

Trinity Church today.

and from Fulton Street to Christopher Street, had belonged to Anneke Jans Bogardus, the widow of the Dutch Reformed Church's dominie, Everardus Bogardus. When Anneke died, in 1663, her children inherited the property. They sold it to the Crown in 1670, and Queen Anne bestowed it on Trinity in 1705. But one of the heirs, Cornelius Bogardus, had failed to sign the deed for the Crown's purchase, and on that ground one of Anneke's hundreds of descendants sued the church in 1833. The courts rejected that claim, but legal actions involving the church's property persisted into the 1950s. The church won them all, and one lawyer who filed such a suit was disbarred, and another was censured.

The "Disturbing" Clergyman

The first Presbyterian clergyman to preach in New York was an Irishman, the Reverend Francis Makemie, who came on a visit in 1707 and was promptly arrested by order of the eccentric, transvestite governor, Lord Cornbury, as a "disturber of government." His defense counsel argued, "We have no established church here. We have liberty of conscience by an act of assembly. . . . This province is made up chiefly of dissenters and persons not of English birth." The Reverend Mr. Makemie won acquittal but the court assessed him the considerable cost of his prosecution—£83.

Clutching a Bible, the Reverend Francis Makemie (left) vigorously defends himself at his trial.

Plaque (above right) indicates landmark status of the present St. Peter's (right), built in 1838.

The First Catholic Church

The oldest Roman Catholic congregation in the city is St. Peter's at Barclay and Church streets, incorporated by act of the legislature in 1785. Its first church building, 48 by 81 feet, was erected in 1786 on five lots purchased from Trinity Church; the Spanish ambassador, Don Diego de Gardoqui, laid the cornerstone. The pastor, the first regularly assigned priest in the New York diocese, was the Reverend Charles Whelan, O.M. Cap., who had been a chaplain in the fleet of the French admiral François de Grasse and had been present at the British surrender at Yorktown. He served at St. Peter's until February 12, 1786, when he left to become a missionary in Kentucky. The present church structure dates from 1838, but the wrought-iron fence around the church and the rectory is older than they are: it was fashioned for Trinity Church in 1790 and donated to St. Peter's in 1846, when Trinity erected its present home.

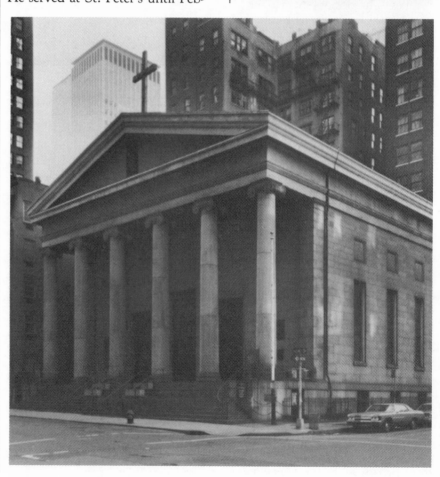

LANDMARKS OF NEW YORK

OLD ST. PETER'S CHURCH

HERE WORSHIPS NEW YORK STATE'S OLDEST ROMAN CATHOLIC PARISH, ORGANIZED IN 1785. THE FIRST CHURCH ON THIS SITE, BUILT A YEAR LATER, REMAINED UNTIL 1836. THE PRESENT BUILDING, WHOSE GREEK REVIVAL DESIGN IS ATTRIBUTED TO ISAIAH ROGERS, WAS BLESSED BY BISHOP JOHN HUGHES IN 1838.

PLAQUE ERECTED 1962 BY
THE NEW YORK COMMUNITY TRUST

The Ex-Slave and His Church

The first exclusively black church, the African Methodist Episcopal Zion Church erected in 1800 at Church and Leonard streets, was largely organized by a former slave named Peter Williams, who had belonged to John Aymar, a Tory tobacconist. When Aymar left the country in 1783, Williams, a patriot, wanted to remain, so he induced the elders of John Street Methodist Church—the city's first Methodist Episcopal Church—to buy him and let him repay the purchase price. (Williams was the church's sexton and undertaker as well as a member of the congregation.) A church document records the transaction: "1783, June 10. Paid Mr. Aymar for his Negro Peter. . . . 40." Williams paid off the £40 in installments in a little more than two years; the final payment was noted thus: "By cash received of Peter Williams, in full of all demands, on the 4th of November 1785. . . . 5." Williams became a Liberty Street businessman and property owner, and he and other successful blacks grew increasingly dissatisfied with what they considered paternalism and

Peter Williams

condescension on the part of the white members of the church. The A.M.E. Zion Church that they established inspired blacks of other denominations to emulate them. Black Baptists organized the Abyssinian Baptist Church in 1809, black Episcopalians St. Philip's Protestant Episcopal Church in 1818, and black Presbyterians the Negro Presbyterian Church in 1821.

Peter Williams's son Peter Jr. became the first black to be ordained in the Episcopal Church; he was St. Philip's first rector.

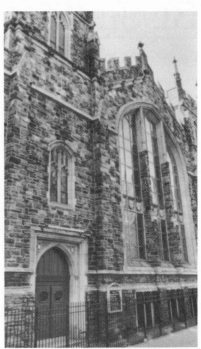

Harlem's Abyssinian Baptist Church, one of the best known of New York's black houses of worship, long constituted the power base of the Reverend Adam Clayton Powell, Jr., who served 11 terms in Congress.

When Peter Williams served as sexton of the John Street church, John Street between William and Nassau streets looked like this.

BUSINESS

Captain Block's Little Craft

The first ship ever built in Manhattan, a sixteen-ton yacht, was completed in the spring of 1614, when the island was not yet settled. The vessel was constructed on the site of Fraunces Tavern by

Using timber felled on the spot, Captain Block and his crew built Onrust *for the trip home.*

Captain Adriaen Block, a fur trader, and his crew after the craft in which they had come, *Tiger,* had burned at its mooring, where the World Trade Center now towers. Block named the yacht *Onrust* (Restless), not for his mood but for a Dutch island that was the last land mariners saw on departing from the Netherlands. Block sailed *Onrust* through Hell Gate and into Long Island Sound, discovered the Connecticut River (which he named Fresh

River to contrast it to the salty Hudson) and circumnavigated Block Island. But *Onrust* was only 44½ feet from stem to stern and 11½ feet of beam, and Block wanted to go home to the Netherlands. So when he encountered the bigger ship *Fortune,* skippered by his friend and fur-trading partner, Captain Hendrick Christaensen, who was in no hurry to return to Europe, they swapped vessels. What happened to *Onrust* is unrecorded. But parts of *Tiger* were discovered in 1916 when a subway was being tunneled through landfill, and the rest lies beneath the World Trade Center.

The Horse-Powered Mill

The city's first mill, which doubled as the first religious meeting place, was built in 1626 by François Fézard (who was generally called François Molemacher, or Molemaeker, meaning millmaker) on the site of 20-22 South William Street. The mill was a one-horsepower affair; one horse tramped in a circle to turn the machinery, which ground pine bark for tanning. The horse had Sunday off, while the townspeople met in the mill's loft to pray. The mill's grindstones survive; in 1835, sixteen of them were dug up behind warehouses in the block bounded by Beaver, Broad, and South William streets, and some are on exhibit at the temple of Shearith Israel—the Spanish and Portuguese Synagogue on Central Park West—and some at the New-York Historical Society. (The temple has the stones because its 1730 forerunner stood where the stones were found.) Four more early millstones were discovered in 1913

Millstone found in 1913 excavation of a Beaver Street backyard hangs on brick exterior wall of church office on West End Avenue. Early mills in the city depended variously on horse-, wind- or water-power.

during excavation of the backyard at 38-40 Beaver Street: three are displayed inside the West End Collegiate Church, at West End Avenue and 77th Street, and the fourth hangs on an outer wall in an alley between the church office and the West End Plaza Hotel, at 378 West End Avenue. The church has the stones because it descends directly from the first religious service in François Fézard's mill, but whether those stones are from the first mill is disputed; Shearith Israel historians contend that they came from a mill built fifty years later at 32-34 South William Street.

The Short-Lived Countinghouse

The city's first office building, erected in 1625, was a stone, reed-thatched countinghouse of the Dutch West India Company on Whitehall Street between Bridge and Pearl streets. Fire destroyed it a few years after its construction.

The Great Ship

The earliest of all Manhattan's grandiose projects, and the first to involve a vast cost overrun, was undertaken in 1631, when New Amsterdam was little more than a half-dozen years old: it was the construction of one of the biggest ships in the world at the time.

The inspiration came from two go-getting Belgian visitors who were shipbuilders themselves. Such a vessel, they told Director General Peter Minuit, would demonstrate the magnificent quality of New Netherland's timber and call attention to New Amsterdam's splendid harbor. Minuit needed little convincing; he said, "Go ahead," and put up Dutch West India Company money to finance the job. Cutting lumber with a horse-powered mill, the Belgians built a vessel that displaced eight hundred tons and carried thirty big guns to discourage privateers and pirates. They named it *New Netherland*, in honor of the smaller *Nieuw Nederland*, which had brought the first settlers in 1624. When the *New Netherland*

reached Europe, it awed everybody except the Dutch West India Company's directors, who were appalled at the size of the construction bills and at the expense of manning the ship. The resulting ruckus contributed to Minuit's dismissal as director general. But government-financed ships—and other projects—still encounter cost overruns.

Construction of boats and ships constituted a major New York industry for some three centuries, and a good many vessels were built at the foot of Maiden Lane, here depicted as it supposedly looked in the 1700s. The craft were launched at the mouth of the stream (center) in which maidens washed the family laundry. Hence the street's name.

The Big Apple's Beginning

The first of the apple orchards for which New York State became famous was planted by Governor Peter Stuyvesant in 1647 on his Bowery Farm; grafts from Stuyvesant's trees, shipped up the Hudson, originated the business that gave upstaters the nickname "appleknockers." A pear tree planted by Stuyvesant at what became the northeast corner of Third Avenue and 13th Street bore fruit for more than two centuries.

Early days "appleknockers," small boys pick the fruit for their sister below to put in baskets.

The Slave Sales Tax

A sales tax, the city's first, was imposed on August 6, 1655, but it applied only to the slave trade. The law, signed by "P. Stuyvesant, Nicasius de Sille, La Montagne," read:

"WHEREAS, the Director General and Council of New Nether-

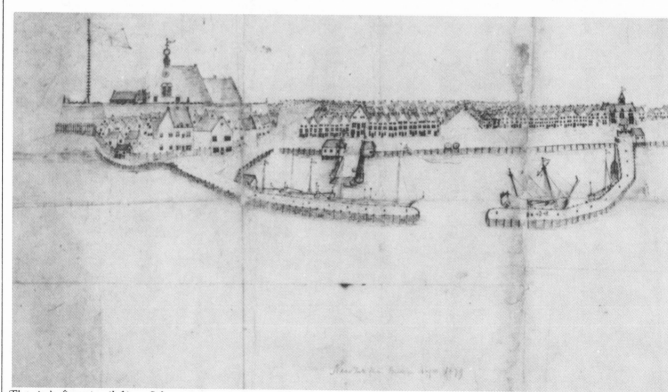

The city's first pier (left) at Schreyers Hook was complemented in 1659 by another (right) that extended from piers and Manhattan's crowded East Moore Street. Looking from Brooklyn Heights, Jasper Danckaerts depicted the River shore in a pen-and-ink drawing included in his Journal of a Voyage to New York, 1679-1680.

land find that the Negroes lately arrived here in the little ship, the *Witte Paert* [White Horse], from the Bight of Guinea, are carried and exported hence, without the Hon[ble] Company, or the Inhabitants of this Province having derived any revenue or benefit thereby, the Director General and Council have resolved and decided that there shall be paid at the General Office on the Negroes who will be carried or exported from here elsewhere beyond the jurisdiction of New Netherland, 10 per cent of what they are worth, or are purchased."

Witte Paert had brought the first slaves direct from Africa, but New Netherland had had slaves for thirty years.

The Tavern and the Horse

The city's first tavern, at the sign of the Wooden Horse, was opened by Philip Geraerdy in 1641 at what became Whitehall and Stone streets. (Before Geraerdy's venture, however, New Amsterdam throats had not been parched: one of every four business establishments sold liquor and beer.) The tavern's name evidenced Geraerdy's sense of the ridiculous. As a militiaman, Geraerdy had been convicted of absence from guard duty and sentenced to ride a wooden horse on parade, with a pitcher in one hand and a drawn sword in the other. That was not so funny as it sounds, for the horse had a sharp spine.

The Pier at Weepers' Point

The city's first pier, a small wooden jetty, was built in the East River in 1648-49, at Schreyers Hook (Weepers' Point) south of what became No. 1 State Street. (Schreyers Hook got its name from Schreyers Toren in Amsterdam, where tearful families stood on the tower—"toren"—and watched as fathers, brothers, and lovers sailed to sea.) The pier was constructed while Peter Stuyvesant was governor, and pictures that show the arriving Stuyvesant marching peg-legged down a pier are imaginative. The Schreyers Hook pier remained the city's only landing until 1659, when another was built at the foot of Moore Street. (Moore Street does not immortalize any Mr. Moore—the name is a corruption of Moor Street, off which ships anchored.)

The Plaints Against Peddlers

Protection against price-cutting peddlers was first granted to local merchants by law on September 18, 1648. The law's preamble read "that several of the Scotch Merchants and Petty Traders who from time to time come over in the ships from Fatherland, do and aim at nothing else than solely to spoil trade and business by their underselling; they dispose of their goods with the utmost speed; give 11 @ 12 guilders in loose Wampum for one Beaver, and when sold out, go back again in the ships of that same year in which they come, without bestowing or conferring any benefit on the Country, all the burthens whereof, on the contrary, the Inhabitants who own property must bear."

The law decreed that "those Merchants, Scots and Petty traders . . . shall not be permitted to carry on any business in the least on shore here unless they take up their abode here in New Netherland three consecutive years, and in addition build in this city New Amsterdam a decent citizen dwelling, each according to his circumstances and means. . . ."

Money of any kind always was welcomed in the city's early days. Coins like this Dutch piece, dated 1686, continued to circulate long after New Amsterdam became New York.

The First Cover-Up

The first big business attempt to conceal a firm's activities was made in 1653. Adriaen van der Donck, the city's first lawyer and the founder of Yonkers, was working on a *Description of New Netherland* and asked the Dutch West India Company directors in Amsterdam for access to the company files here. The directors wrote to Governor Peter Stuyvesant instructing him to let Van der Donck "have such documents and papers as may be thought of service to him in completing his history," but to "be cautious that the company's own weapons may not be used against us and we be drawn into new troubles and quarrels."

The Business on the Bridge

The first merchants' exchange, forerunner of all of New York's commodity and stock exchanges, began doing business in 1670, when Dutch and English craftsmen, importers, traders, and merchants met on Fridays between 11 a.m. and noon on a bridge spanning a canal at Bridge Street, at that time called Brugh Street. The sessions were organized by Colonel Sir Francis Lovelace, the British governor who had taken command in 1668.

Survivors of the city's past, 18th-century buildings (left) on Bridge Street are dwarfed by modern structures nearby. The old bridge has vanished.

The printing office and stationer's shop of Robert Bowne was re-created in Water Street near its original site. As this book went to press, the shop was being closed down because of major construction at the South Street Seaport.

The Patent That Washington Signed

The nation's first patent was issued in New York City on July 31, 1790, and bore the signatures of President Washington, Attorney General Edmund Randolph, and Secretary of State Thomas Jefferson. Granted to Samuel Hopkins of Philadelphia for fourteen years, the patent involved a process for making and purifying potash, which was used in soapmaking.

The Persistent Printer

The oldest New York firm still doing business under its original name is Bowne & Company, which Robert Bowne, printer and stationer, established in 1775 at what was then 39 Queen Street (now the corner of Pearl and Fulton streets). The company has added an "Inc." to its name, its headquarters are at 345 Hudson Street, and its operations are nationwide. But in conjunction with the South Street Seaport Museum it has opened an old-fashioned printer's and stationer's shop at 211 Water Street, close by Robert Bowne's old place, and sets type there just as Bowne did.

LAWS

No Tennis on Sunday

The first Sunday law, which forbade drinking during church hours, was passed on April 11, 1641. But New Amsterdamers violated it so offhandedly that a stronger ordinance was voted on October 26, 1656. Among the second law's prohibitions were playing tennis, going for a ride in a cart, and dancing. The ordinance, the preamble of which sounded a plaintive note, read:

"The Director General and Council of New Netherland,

"To all those who hear or see these Presents read, Greeting, make known.

"That it is found by daily and sad experience, that the previously issued and frequently renewed Ordinances and Edicts against the desecration of the Lord's Sabbath . . . are, to the dishonor of God . . . neither regarded, observed, maintained nor even enforced. . . . Therefore, the Director and Council aforesaid . . . hereby interdict and forbid,

"First, all persons from performing or doing on the Lord's day of rest, by us called Sunday, any ordinary labor, such as Ploughing, Sowing, Mowing, building, Woodsawing, Smithing, Bleaching, Hunting, Fishing or any other work which may be lawful on other days, on pain of forfeiting One pound Flemish for each person; much less any lower or unlawful exercise and Amusement, Drunkenness, frequenting Taverns or Tippling Houses, Dancing, playing Ball, Cards, Tricktrack, Tennis, Cricket or Ninepins, going on pleasure parties in a Boat, Cart or Wagon before, between or during Divine Service on pain of a double fine; especially all Tavern-keepers, or Tapsters from en-

Bowling, one of the diversions that the early settlers preferred to church-going, retained its popularity during the British regime; while their ladies watched, gentlemen played the game, as this etching dating to about 1765 records, on what New York still officially designates as Bowling Green.

Like bowling and other recreations, drinking on Sunday was proscribed under Dutch law but since the city's second decade, taverns have never been lacking. This one, pictured in 1784—the first year of post-Revolutionary peace—stood on the north side of Wall Street just a few hundred feet east of the ruins of the first Trinity Church.

tertaining any Clubs, or tapping, bestowing, giving or selling directly any Brandy, Wine, Beer or Strong Liquor to any person before, between or during the Sermons, under a fine of six guilders to be forfeited by the Tavern-keeper or Tapster for each person and three guilders by every person found drinking at the time aforesaid. . . ." At the current rate of exchange, a guilder is half a dollar.

The Anti-Speeding Law

The first law against speeding was passed on June 27, 1652. It provided that "in order to prevent accidents . . . no Wagons, Carts, Sleighs shall be run, rode or driven at a gallop within this city," and required drivers to walk beside and lead their horses, except on Broadway. Violators were subject to a fine of "two pounds Flemish for the first time, and for the second time double, and for the third time to be arbitrarily corrected therefor and in addition to be responsible for all damages which may arise therefrom."

Banned except on Broadway.

The No-Shooting-in-the-Streets Law

The first gun-control law was passed on October 9, 1652; it put the city off-limits to hunters, forbidding the firing of guns at "Partridges or other Game . . . on pain of forfeiting the gun and a fine at the discretion of the Judge, to be applied one-third to the Poor, one-third to the Church and one-third to the Officer." The law explained that "complaints already have been made" against the daily discharge of weapons, by which "People or Cattle might perhaps be struck and injured."

> *Without any price-control law, bread was cheaper in Bleecker Street in 1937 than it had been in New Amsterdam under Governor Peter Stuyvesant.*

The Price-of-Bread Law

The first price-fixing law for the protection of consumers was passed on October 26, 1656. Governor Peter Stuyvesant and his council did "hereby Ordain and command that all Bakers and all other Inhabitants who make a business of baking or selling Bread, whether for Christians or Barbarians, shall be obliged, as well for the accommodation of Christians as to derive profit thereby from Indians, to bake at least once or twice a week both coarse and white Bread, as well for Christians as Indians, of the stated weight and at the price, as follows:

"The Coarse loaf shall weigh:
"The double, 8 lb., and cost 14 stivers.
The single, 4 lb., and cost 7 stivers.
The half, 2 lb., and cost 3½ stivers.

"The White loaf shall weigh:
"The double, 2 lb., and cost 8 stivers.
The single, 1 lb., and cost 4 stivers.
The half, ½ lb., and cost 2 stivers."

(A stiver was worth about two cents.)

A previous law had forbidden the sale of white bread because only the Indians had enough wampum to buy it.

GOVERNORS

The First Elected Governor

The first fully empowered governor of New Amsterdam (or, correctly, at the time, Fort Amsterdam) and of New Netherland was Peter Minuit, but it is a rare New Yorker who knows more about him than that he purchased Manhattan from the Indians. Yet Minuit exemplified the dynamism and cosmopolitanism that became characteristic of New York. He was German by birth—his parents were religious refugees in Wesel, Rhenish Prussia, when he was born in 1580. He was French of name and probably of French-speaking, Belgian Walloon stock. (Minuit means "midnight" in French.) And he was Dutch by residence and citizenship.

Though encyclopedias and history books have it that he first arrived here on May 4, 1626, under appointment by the Dutch West India Company as the colony's director general, or governor, little-known records indicate a different story. Minuit came in a minor capacity a year or two ear-

lier; Dutch West India Company instructions to William ver Hulst, Minuit's predecessor, assert that "he shall have Pierre Minuyt as volunteer . . . and others whom he deems competent thereto to sail up the [Hudson] river as far as they can." The instructions are believed to have been issued in January, 1625.

But Ver Hulst was shipped home and, according to a letter to Amsterdam written by Isaack de Rasieres, the colony's secretary, Minuit was elected governor by a council of the settlers. (Minuit thus became the city's first popularly chosen official.) Presumably Minuit returned to the Netherlands for confirmation in the post, got it, and returned to Fort Amsterdam in May of 1626. A stickler for propriety and determined to legalize the Dutch presence on Manhattan, he assembled Indian chiefs and their squaws

A squaw covetously eyes an imported blouse as Peter Minuit displays to assembled Indian chiefs and warriors the goods he offers to exchange for Manhattan Island.

sometime between July and September and negotiated to buy the island for 60 guilders—or $30, at current exchange rates—in goods. (It was a sizable sum—the price of a round-trip transatlantic passage.) He immediately got under way the construction of thirty houses, a warehouse, gristmills, sawmills, and a mill to grind bark for tanning. He built a blockhouse for shelter from attack. The following year he initiated trade talks with the English colony at Plymouth, Massachusetts. By 1631, he had the bustling community financing and hammering together one of the world's greatest ships of its time, an eight-hundred-ton craft called *New Netherland* in commemoration of the smaller vessel that had brought the first settlers (see page 8). Despite his accomplishments, the Dutch West India Company fired him that same year, 1631; he was too generous, the company feared, in granting trading privileges to the patroons, investors to whom the company had allocated vast tracts of land, and thus was endangering the company's trade monopoly.

Jobless at age fifty-one, Minuit finally joined the Swedish West India Company. For the Swedes, he sailed two ships to Delaware, where he bought from the Indians (for a copper pot, one story goes) a huge area that included the present Delaware château country; in March, 1638, he established a colony of Swedes and Finns near the site of Wilmington.

Three months later, on a business trip to the West Indies, Minuit boarded the Dutch ship *Vliegend Hert* (Flying Deer) in the harbor of St. Kitts to visit its captain. A sudden storm blew the ship to sea, and neither the vessel nor Minuit was ever heard from again.

The First Corrupt Governor

The first governor to make public office a private trust was Wouter van Twiller, who started the practice in 1633, when the city was only nine years old. A crewcut, hog-heavy little fellow who had clerked in the Dutch West India Company's Amsterdam warehouse, Van Twiller wangled his post here after marrying a niece of Kiliaen van Rensselaer, an influential Amsterdamer who owned land up the Hudson but who never visited America. Soon after arriving, in April of 1633, Van Twiller as director general, or governor, deeded Van Twiller as private citizen several hundred acres of Greenwich Village tobacco farmland that Peter Minuit, a predecessor, had set aside for the company. Then Van Twiller acquired Nutten (now Governors) Island, two East River islands, and a share in fifteen thousand acres in Flatlands, in Brooklyn. When the public prosecutor, Lubbertus van Dincklagen, made disapproving noises, Van Twiller fired him and sent him home to the Netherlands, a prisoner, without the three years' pay due him.

But Van Dincklagen blew the whistle in Amsterdam, won Van Twiller's dismissal in 1637, and himself became assistant director general here. The Dutch West India Company took back much of the land that Van Twiller had bestowed on himself, but he stayed on in the colony—its wealthiest citizen.

Viewed from Brooklyn Heights (foreground) in the early 1800s, Governors Island still abounded in the chestnut, oak and hickory trees that thrived there when Wouter van Twiller owned it.

The First Governor to Be Hanged

Almost three hundred years have passed since the chill, drizzly dawn of May 16, 1691, when a German clergyman's son named Jacob Leisler was led to the gallows at Broadway and Chambers Street—the only governor of New York ever to be hanged. Yet, among the relatively rare folk who still recognize the name, the conflicting passions that attended his execution and that of his son-in-law Jacob Milborne hotly persist. The writer of this book, for example, was engaged in conversation not long ago by a stranger sitting next to him in a New York theater. The stranger, who introduced himself as a visiting Californian, asked the author what he did for a living. The writer said that at the moment he was working on a book about New York's past. The Californian shot back, "Do you believe Leisler was guilty?" The writer replied that he did not. "Of course not!" said the visitor, relaxing. Soon afterward, an editor read the foregoing. "How can you say that?" she expostulated. "The man was a murderer and a tyrant!" In Leisler's time, all New York was similarly rent: one cheered him in the streets and later sobbed and shrieked as he died, or one met secretly with others of his foes to plot his fall.

The dark drama in which Leisler played the leading role began quietly enough in 1660 when Leisler arrived in New Netherland from Frankfort-am-Main as a twenty-five-year-old soldier in the service of the Dutch West India Company. When England seized the colony in 1664, Leisler supported the new government, as did many of the city's residents. He became a merchant, wine importer, and shipping entrepreneur, and augmented his growing fortune by marrying Elsje Tymens, widow of the wealthy Pieter van der Veen; his marriage related him to the aristocratic Bayards and Van Cortlandts and, though he was rough in speech and manner, ranked him socially with the upper classes. Ten years after his arrival as a common soldier, he became an elder of the Dutch church and subsequently senior captain of the militia.

The winds that were to propel him to the gallows swirled up in 1688, when England's Roman Catholic King James II was overthrown, and William and Mary, the Protestant Prince and Princess of Orange, were proclaimed King and Queen of England. The news posed a problem for New York: Who was in charge? Were King James's appointees to govern until they were replaced by William and Mary? Or should the people meanwhile govern themselves? The issue was far from academic. Religious antipathies at the time rivaled those of modern Ulster. If James's appointees retained office, Protestants feared, would they not attempt to save the colony for the deposed king? Such fears were heightened when Francis Nicholson, the lieutenant governor, declared intemperately that he would rather see the city burn than take orders from representatives of the populace. Rumors of horrendous conspiracies flew. Importuned by members of his militia company, Leisler reluctantly moved into the fort from which Nicholson had governed; Nicholson yielded his authority, and the militia captains then signed a document, prepared by Leisler, that they would jointly run the government until they heard from William and Mary. Nicholson departed.

Belatedly, a letter arrived from William, addressed to "Our Trusty and well beloved Francis Nicholson, Esquire, our Lieutenant Governor of our Province of New York in America, or in his absence, to such as for the time being take care to keep the peace and Administer the Laws of our

Scene of Leisler's hanging at Broadway and Chambers Street is dominated by the Municipal Building (background).

said Province." It authorized the recipient to take charge until the king sent a new governor.

Leisler had emerged, by force of his personality, as the leader of the anti-Jamesites; he had, in fact, been elected commander-in-chief of the colony by a Committee of Safety. Now he was persuaded by his followers—who undoubtedly represented a majority of the citizens—to assume that the royal letter was meant for him. During the thirteen months of his governorship, New York City got its first popularly elected mayor, sheriff, aldermen, and councilmen, and Leisler demonstrated a good deal of skill at administration, raising money to finance the government, establishing courts, and keeping the peace. The peace indeed needed keeping, for riots kept erupting, but Leisler quieted them without anyone's being killed. However, his powers never extended beyond the region of the city, despite his title of lieutenant governor, and within the city he was never unchallenged, for he had bitter enemies. Roughly and in a gross over-simplification, Leisler's supporters represented a Protestant populism, and his opponents constituted a wealthy Roman Catholic aristocracy. But families, friends, churches, and neighborhoods were sharply divided for reasons that blurred the lines of religion, race, or class. Leisler's governing council, for example, included substantial citizens of English, Dutch, and French origin, and his followers numbered—along with a violent rabble—highly respectable churchmen, militia captains, and prosperous merchants.

What eventually doomed Leisler was a combination of his own obstinacy and self-righteousness and the personal as well as political enmity of one of his kinsmen

Sword upraised, Jacob Leisler leads a party of his supporters along Pearl Street to take command of the fort from Lieutenant Governor Nicholson.

by marriage, Nicholas Bayard, with whom Leisler had quarreled over property. His obstinacy manifested itself when a new lieutenant governor, Richard Ingoldesby, arrived to take command of New York, and demanded that Leisler turn over the fort. But Ingoldesby lacked written orders from the new king—the documents were on a ship that had been delayed in a storm. Leisler refused to yield his authority without them. A clash of arms between Ingoldesby's troops and Leisler's militia ensued, and a few of Ingoldesby's soldiers were killed.

A couple of days later, the documents arrived, along with Colonel Henry Sloughter, an impecunious adventurer whom William and Mary had named governor of New York. Bayard and some of his followers persuaded Sloughter that Leisler was a rebel and a traitor; Leisler and his son-in-law were arrested, and a stacked court convicted them of treason and murder, the second charge having been based on the deaths of Ingoldesby's soldiers. The two men were sentenced "to be hanged by the neck, and being alive," to be

cut down, drawn and quartered, and their heads "to be severed from their bodies."

Sloughter, wary of executing the first man to take leadership here on behalf of William and Mary, refused to carry out the sentence. Bayard and other enemies of Leisler then got Sloughter drunk at a party, and, it is suspected, slipped him a bribe to sign the death warrants. Before Sloughter sobered up, Leisler and Milborne were led to the gallows. Leisler's last words were "I forgive my enemies as I hope to be forgiven and I entreat my children to do the same."

As a horde of onlookers wept and shrieked, the sentence was carried out. What remained of Leisler's and Milborne's bodies was buried in Leisler's garden, in

Disinterred remains of Jacob Leisler are borne to the old Dutch church in Bowling Green after Leisler's exoneration by the Parliament in London.

what is now Nassau Street. Two months later, Sloughter himself died unexpectedly; he was said by Leisler's mourners to have committed suicide out of remorse, and by Leisler's enemies to have been poisoned. But six doctors, after conducting New York's first autopsy, determined that he had drunk himself to death.

Four years later, Parliament in London reversed Leisler's and Milborne's convictions. And on a stormy midnight in October, 1698, with a hundred soldiers forming a guard of honor, Leisler and Milborne were disinterred. A vast, torchlit procession of mourners, to the beat of muffled drums, accompanied the coffins through the rain, wind, and darkness to the City Hall. The bodies lay in state for several days, then were reinterred in a crypt in the old Dutch church on Bowling Green.

Had William Shakespeare still lived, he might well have scripted the travail of Jacob Leisler into one of his major tragedies.

The First Publicity-Conscious Governor

The first governor to put his name on a public work was Willem Kieft, who hoped to immortalize himself by means of a marble slab that he affixed to the elaborate church built in 1642 on the site of Bowling Green (see page 30). When the church was demolished ninety-nine years later, the slab disappeared in the mud; rediscovered, it was attached to a new church, which was destroyed in the great fire of 1835. The slab then vanished forever, and Kieft is remembered, if at all, for his unprovoked wars against the Indians.

The First Catholic Governor

New York's first Roman Catholic governor was Colonel Thomas Dongan, an Irishman whose arrival here in the company of a Jesuit priest on April 25, 1683, was attended by suspicion and foreboding on the part of the overwhelmingly Protestant citizenry. But his fairness, honesty, and courtesy quickly won him wide popularity, and his liberal views, extreme for his time, were later to influence the New York State and United States constitutions.

Appointed by the Duke of York, a convert to Catholicism who owned the province, Dongan came with instructions to give New Yorkers a measure of political and religious liberty. Political liberty, the Duke hoped, would make the restive colonists more amenable to paying taxes; religious liberty, the Duke secretly intended, would allow him to establish Catholicism as the colony's major faith. Dongan promptly promulgated a Charter of Liberties and Privileges that provided for a more or less popularly elected General Assembly, forbade taxation without the Assembly's consent, established trial by jury, and granted freedom of worship to all Christians. It was more than the Duke had bargained for—when he became King James II, in 1685, he reluctantly signed the charter, but he never returned it to New York; technically it lapsed, but philosophically, it has survived.

Charter or not, Dongan pursued his own course. He went to Mass—the first ever celebrated openly in New York—on October 30, 1683, but he defied James's orders to extend Catholicism's influence in the province and

The seal on Governor Dongan's charter for the Province of New York was inscribed Honi Soit Qui Mal Y Pense, *motto of the Order of the Garter.*

surrounded himself with Protestant advisers to allay the people's fears of a Catholic takeover. When James instructed him not to interfere if the French sent down an expedition from Quebec to exterminate the Indians, Dongan tipped off the tribes to the planned massacre. He negotiated with the Indians, neighboring colonies, and Canada to fix New York's boundaries. He established charters for New York City and Albany.

For his good behavior, King James fired him in 1688 and he retired to his 5,100-acre estate on Staten Island, where Dongan Hills is named for him and Castleton Avenue for his home, which he called Cassiltowne, after his birthplace in Ireland. He was not to enjoy his retirement; when James was replaced on the English throne by the Protestant William and Mary, persecution of Catholics compelled Dongan to seek refuge in New England; several years later he returned to England, and eventually succeeded his brother as Earl of Limerick. But his family's lands had been confiscated, and he died a poor man at the age of eighty-one.

The Transvestite Governor

The first, and presumably the only, transvestite governor that New York has had successively impressed, amused, bewildered, and finally infuriated the city's residents during his tenure, from 1702 to 1708. He was Edward Hyde, Lord Cornbury, and he arrived with imposing credentials. He was a cousin of England's Queen Anne, he had been a Member of Parliament for sixteen years, and he was a veteran army officer who had endeared himself to King William III—Anne's predecessor—by deserting his (Cornbury's) uncle King James II to support the Protestant William. Furthermore, he had married well: his wife, Katherine, was Baroness Clifton of Leighton Bromwold, daughter of Lord O'Brien and heiress to the Most Noble Charles, Duke of Richmond and Lenox. He was even a good family man, it seemed, for he had sired seven children.

New Yorkers were somewhat taken aback, then, when at a welcoming banquet Cornbury devoted his speech to praising the beauty of his wife's ears and insisted that each male guest feel them for himself. The citizens were quite bewildered, soon afterward, when Cornbury himself gave a grandiose ball and charged admittance; some of the invited guests refused to pay and huffily went home.

Cornbury's behavior seemed odder still when he began dressing in his wife's gowns and, berouged and bepowdered, flounced daily along the parapets of the fort he commanded, while his sentries smirked. On occasion he sallied along Broadway, where at least once he was arrested and hauled back to the fort; one night, when a patrolling watch-man investigated the presence of an apparent prostitute stumbling about the fort, the "prostitute"—Cornbury—leaped at him, giggling, and pulled his ears. Unperturbed by the gossip that the incident—and similar incidents that frightened night-strolling

Lord Cornbury sat for his portrait dressed like an aristocratic woman and often wore clothes appropriated from his wife. An explanation at the time was that he fancied his resemblance to his cousin, Queen Anne, England's monarch.

citizens—provoked, Cornbury posed for his portrait in a low-necked dress, holding a fan and wearing a bit of lace in his hair.

But New Yorkers were generally a tolerant lot and eccentricities were the privilege of the English nobility. What most irritated people was Cornbury's penchant for borrowing money from everyone—who could refuse a governor?—and never paying it back.

Lady Cornbury, for her part, proved a suitable consort. Corn-

bury had chosen her as his bride from among a bevy of available belles because he had fallen in love with her ears; at the wedding, he kissed them rather than her mouth. In New York, though, Cornbury's passion waned and he cut off Her Ladyship's pin money. Since he wore her clothes and she could not buy any, she borrowed and never returned the gowns of the aristocratic women on whom she called; a dozen friends served as seamstresses to alter the clothes to fit. For her other needs, she simply appropriated anything that struck her fancy: when her carriage—the only one in town—was heard approaching, every hostess ordered the servants to hide the silver and china. (Often that did

Overlooking the Hudson, Franklin D. Roosevelt's beloved Hyde Park gets its name from Cornbury's—Edward Hyde.

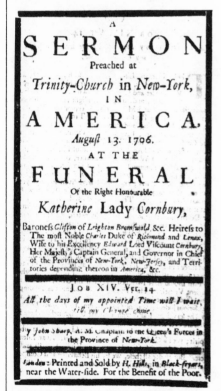

A SERMON Preached at Trinity-Church in New-York, IN AMERICA. August 13. 1706. AT THE FUNERAL Of the Right Honourable Katherine Lady Cornbury,

Baroness *Clifton of Leighton Bromswold*, &c. Heiress to The most Noble *Charles* Duke of *Richmond* and *Lenox*, Wife to his Excellency *Edward* Lord Viscount *Cornbury*, Her Majesty's Captain General, and Governor in Chief of the Provinces of *New-York*, *New-Jersey*, and Territories depending thereon in *America*, &c.

JOB XIV. Ver. 14
All the days of my appointed Time will I wait, till my Change come.

By *John Sharp*, A. M. Chaplain to the Queen's Forces in the Province of *New-York*.

London : Printed and Sold by H. Hills, in *Black-fryars*, near the Water-side. For the Benefit of the Poor.

A curious contribution to charity, the pamphlet that preserves the sermon delivered at Lady Cornbury's funeral runs to 16 pages of small type. How well it sold, the publishers did not say.

not avail; the next day Her Ladyship would send for things she had missed.)

Lady Cornbury died here, at the age of thirty-four, in August, 1706, and her husband, characteristically, charged the cost of her funeral at Trinity Church, where she is buried, to the taxpayers. But the text of the funeral sermon, which filled sixteen pages of small type and was, tactfully, devoted entirely to the fourteenth chapter of Job, was printed as a pamphlet and sold in London "for the benefit of the poor."

Cornbury's persistent peccadilloes and peculations—he used tax moneys as his own—and complaints about them from New York finally led Queen Anne to replace him in 1708. He was about to board ship and stealthily

depart when his creditors caught up with him and had the sheriff toss him into debtors' prison, where he spent the next year. But the death of his father, the Earl of Clarendon, provided him with enough money to pay off most of what he owed. He returned to England, and took his seat in the House of Lords. (What he wore to its sessions is not recorded.)

Fortunately for Cornbury, Queen Anne proved both forgiving and generous: in 1711, she elevated him to the Privy Council and in 1714 appointed him her Envoy Extraordinary—a fitting title—to Hanover. He died in 1723. The most widely detested governor in the city's history, he is commemorated here, ironically, in the name of Franklin D. Roosevelt's family estate, Hyde Park: for an appropriate under-the-table payment, Cornbury had bestowed a grant to the land on some pals, and they christened the place for him.

ENVIRONMENT

The Anti-Air Pollution Act

The first clean-air act was passed by the City Council on February 10, 1797. It provided that after July 1 "no person shall dress sheep or lamb skins, or manufacture glue, nor shall any soap-boiler, or tallow-chandler, or starch-maker, or maker or dresser of vellum, carry on any of their processes or operations of their said trades, which produce impure air, or offensive smells, such as trying or melting of fat or tallow, boiling soap, fermenting grain, or other substances for starch, washing, fermenting or oiling skins, or vellum, at any place within the city of New-York, south of the south side of Grant [Grand] Street, and of the south side of the said street continued until it intersects the easterly side of Mulberry-street, and south of the west line, from the intersection afore-said, continued to Hudson's river." But soap- and candle-makers protested so vehemently that they won exemption from the ban, provided they kept their plants inoffensive.

Air pollution was a problem even in 1787, when Peter T. Curtenius's iron works (above), which produced Franklin stoves, pots and kettles and dozens of other items, belched black smoke over the city. Soap factories, another source of nuisance, were regulated by law in 1797, but the rules did not apply to do-it-yourself operations (below).

The Zoning Law

The city's first zoning law was adopted in 1916; it was motivated by construction of the Equitable Building at 120 Broadway, which crowded 1.2 million square feet of floor space onto a little less than an acre.

The No-Smoking Ordinance

The first city ordinance forbidding smoking in public was passed January 21, 1908, but it applied only to women: it required managers of public establishments to restrain female smokers. A similar proposed ordinance had been defeated earlier by the Board of Aldermen because it would have proscribed smoking by men in the presence of women.

In a sardonic comment on turn-of-the-century smoking customs, the artist Charles Dana Gibson titled his picture "In Leap Year: The Gentlemen Leave the Ladies to Their Tobacco and Wine."

The Anti-Litter Law

The first anti-litter and anti-public nuisance act was passed June 7, 1644. It read:

"The Honble Director General and Council of New Netherland having observed that Soldiers and others residing in Fort Amsterdam, deposit ashes and other filth within the Fort. We, therefore, make known unto all and every one that from now henceforward Ashes and other dirt shall be conveyed outside the Fort, and

that no one shall make water within the Fort, and if any one be caught by the sentinel in the act, he shall pay to him or the Provost three stivers [fifteen Dutch cents, worth about a U.S. nickel], and if he refuse to pay, the sentinel or Provost shall be empowered to levy execution on the offenders."

Whether the ordinance proved any more effective than the current regulations against littering has not been determined.

SOCIAL CUSTOMS

Divorce, Indian Fashion

The first study and report on Manhattan divorces were made by Isaack de Rasieres, who was named New Netherland's secretary in 1626. De Rasieres wrote: "When a [Indian] woman here addicts herself to fornication, and the husband comes to know of it, he thrashes her soundly, and if he wishes to get rid of her, he summons the Sackima [Sachem] with her friends, before whom he accuses her; and if she be found guilty the Sackima commands one

Sachem of the Maquaas, or Mohawks, Sa Ga Yeath Oua Pieth Tow qualified to preside as judge in divorce suits among his tribesmen. He was one of four sachems presented in London in 1710 to Queen Anne, who had their portraits painted by I. Verelst.

to cut off her hair in order that she may be held up before the world as a whore, which they call *poerochque*; and then the husband takes from her everything that she has and drives her out of the house; if there be children, they remain with her, for they are fond of them beyond measure. . . . And when a man is unfaithful, the wife accuses him before the Sackima, which most frequently happens when the wife has a preference for another man. The husband being found guilty, the wife is permitted to draw off his right shoe and left stocking (which they make of deer or elk skins, which they know how to prepare very broad and soft and wear in the winter time); she then tears off the lappet that covers his private parts, gives him a kick behind, and so drives him out of the house; and then 'Adam' scampers off."

De Rasieres also reported on the use of a supposed aphrodisiac. Writing to a friend in Amsterdam, he noted that the Indians prized "a sort of white salmon, which is of very good flavor . . . It has white scales; the heads are so full of fat that in some there are two or three spoonfuls, so that there is good eating for one who is fond of picking heads. It seems that this fish makes them lascivious, for it is often observed that those who have caught any when they have gone fishing, have given them, on their return, to the women, who look for them anxiously." The settlers apparently tried the fish, too, for De Rasieres added, "Our people also confirm this."

The First Servant Problem

The first complaint about the servant problem was put in writing in 1628. The city's first clergyman, the Reverend Jonas Michaëlius, whose wife died soon after the family's arrival in April of that year, wrote home in August: "I find myself by the loss of my good and helpful partner very much hindered and distressed—for my two little daughters are yet small; maid servants are not here

The Reverend Jonas Michaëlius's little daughters probably looked and dressed much like this 17th-century Dutch child painted by Bartholomeus van der Helst sometime before 1670.

to be had, at least none whom they can advise me to take; and the Angola slave women are thievish, lazy and useless trash. The young man whom I took with me I discharged after Whitsuntide, for the reason that I could not employ him out-of-doors at any working of the land, and in-doors he was a burden to me instead of an assistance."

The Dutch Girl And the Dane

The first suit for breach of promise to marry was filed in 1653 by Pieter Laurenzen Kock, a Dane who owned a tavern at No. 1 Broadway. The defendant was Annetje van Vorst, a more than normally stubborn Dutch girl who was the daughter of Kock's longtime business partner in the fur trade, Cornelis van Vorst. Van Vorst was all for the marriage, but when he died Annetje broke the engagement. The burgomasters and *schepens* (*schepen* can be translated as alderman, magistrate, or sheriff) who tried the case stalled for a year before sagely deciding that, "the promise of marriage having been made and given before the Eyes of God," it had to remain in force but did not have to be fulfilled. Instead, neither Pieter nor Annetje was to marry anyone else without being released by the other from the engagement. Annetje was permitted to keep Kock's presents and the two were to share the cost of the suit. Presumably, Kock yielded, because on November 11, 1656, Annetje announced her forthcoming marriage to Claes Janszen, a Dutchman from the old country. And Kock announced on June 13, 1657, that he was engaged to Anneken Dircks of Amsterdam. He died three years later.

Early residents of what is now New York lived comfortably and even elegantly, despite the fact that they were pioneers, at least by the calendar.

This is the dining room of Jan Martense Schenk's house in Flatbush as it looked in 1675 and looks now in the Brooklyn Museum.

GHOSTS AND GRAVES

Trinity Churchyard's Empty Grave

Just a few paces insde the handsome wrought-iron picket fence that separates Trinity Churchyard from Broadway lies a mystery-shrouded grave that contains no bones; the name CHARLOTTE TEMPLE incised on its weathered tombstone is that of a character in a novel. But for much of the nineteenth century and well into the twentieth the grave was watered with tears and decked with flowers by Charlotte's mourners; the *New York Sun* of November 5, 1931, reported that a hundred and fifty years after Charlotte's creation fresh roses still appeared regularly on that grave, and *The New York Times* of November 11, 1955, said, "Trinity Church reports constant inquiries for the location of the grave."

"When I was a boy, the story of Charlotte Temple was familiar in the household of every New Yorker," an attorney who had spent all of his seventy years in the vicinity of Trinity Church wrote to the *New York Evening Post* in 1903. "The first tears I ever saw in the eyes of a grown person were shed for her. In that churchyard are heroes, philosophers and martyrs, whose names are familiar to the youngest scholar and whose memory is dear to the wisest and best. Their graves, tho' marked by imposing monuments, win but a glance of curiosity while the turf over Charlotte Temple is kept fresh by falling tears." A nineteenth-century history of New York City refers to "the unfortunate Charlotte Temple" without amplification, apparently on the assumption that none was needed.

Hoax or historic relic, tombstone engraved with the name Charlotte Temple lies in Trinity Churchyard.

The novel that evoked the tears was *Charlotte: A Tale of Truth*, the author of which signed herself simply "Mrs. Rowson." First published in England in 1790 and in America in 1794, the book went into some two hundred editions—many of them pirated—and before Harriet Beecher Stowe's *Uncle Tom's Cabin* appeared, it flourished as the greatest best-seller in American publishing history. (Funk & Wagnalls released a definitive, annotated version in 1905, and an English first edition sold in New York in 1955 for more than $5,000.)

Mrs. Rowson's tale was simple. A few years before the Revolutionary War, a beautiful upper-class fifteen-year-old English schoolgirl—Charlotte—is urged by a handsome British army officer, one Montraville, to accompany him to America, where he will marry her. Influenced by her instructor in French, a Mlle. La Rue—who has a shady past and has been bribed by Montraville—Charlotte agrees. After a brief, illicit idyll in New York, Montraville abandons Charlotte and marries a local heiress. Not entirely a villain, Montraville entrusts a fellow-officer with money for Charlotte, but the friend fails to deliver it. Charlotte, evicted from the love nest, dies in poverty after giving birth to a daughter, just as her father, a clergyman, arrives from England to succor her. He buries her in an unmarked grave in Trinity Churchyard and returns to England with Charlotte's child, Lucy.

Charlotte's tragedy does not end with her death; it haunts Lucy and Montraville for the rest of their lives. In *Lucy Temple*, a sequel to *Charlotte*, Mrs. Rowson relates that Lucy, on her twenty-first birthday, becomes engaged to a young army lieutenant and, on the same day, receives as a gift a miniature portrait of her mother. The lieutenant simultaneously hears that his father, a colonel, is dying and, because the portrait so strongly resembles Lucy, borrows it to show to him. On seeing the picture, the dying man cries out, "It is . . . it is come again to blast my vision in my last hour. The woman you would marry is my own daughter. Just Heaven! Oh, that I could have been spared this!" He really wasn't a bad fellow, Mrs. Rowson indicates, describing him as being "of patient, noble and generous feeling—a promise of everything that was excellent in character and desirable in fortune—all blighted by once yielding to the impulses of guilty passion." Lucy never marries.

Sad tales indeed, but hardly

Susanna Haswell Rowson, as she appears in a miniature owned by her descendants.

enough to induce a century-long flow of tears. What moved New Yorkers was Mrs. Rowson's subtitle, *A Tale of Truth*, and the conviction that there once were a Charlotte, a Montraville, and a Lucy and that the real Charlotte once lay in Trinity Churchyard. Mrs. Rowson, who became a distinguished editor, writer, and educator in Boston, said—years after she had written her novels—that Charlotte Temple actually was Charlotte Stanley, daughter of the Earl of Derby's younger son, an impecunious Anglican clergyman. (The clergyman was poor because, in defiance of the custom of the time, he had married for love rather than money.) Mrs. Rowson's Montraville, she confided, was her own cousin, Colonel (or Captain) John Montrésor, of the Royal Engineers. A highly regarded soldier, he had fought beside George Washington in the disastrous pre-Revolutionary battle at Fort Duquesne; he was also an artist and cartographer, and had prepared the 1775 map of New York City. From 1772 to 1777, he owned Randalls Island (then known as Montrésor's Is-

land), abandoning it only when his estate there burned down, presumably with help from American forces.

Few challenged Mrs. Rowson's account. In answer to the question "What is the basis of Mrs. Rowson's novel of Charlotte Temple?"—put to *The New York Times Saturday Review* by "L.F." of Westbrook, Connecticut—the editor responded on February 7, 1903, "Mrs. Rowson founded her novel on the career of Charlotte Stanley, the mistress of Captain John Montrésor, who died about 1776 in the Old Tree House, at Pell and Doyers Street, New York City, and is buried in Trinity Churchyard. Montrésor is the Montraville of the novel. Mrs.

Illustrations for one of the 200 or so editions of Charlotte Temple *show her eloping and then languishing while awaiting a visit from her lover*

Rowson, we believe, was a relative of his." Other newspapers provided similar responses whenever the question popped up, as it frequently did.

Despite Mrs. Rowson, could Montrésor have been her Montraville? The evidence to the contrary is formidable:

Montrésor spent twenty-three years—from 1755 to 1778—in military service in America, with one six-months' home leave in 1766, when Charlotte, by the novel's chronology, was six or seven years old.

Montrésor did not marry a New York heiress—whom the novel calls Julia Franklin—after his supposed seduction of Charlotte. On March 1, 1764, he married Frances Tucker, the daughter of Thomas Tucker, of Tucker's Town, Bermuda, and fathered ten children by her. (Eight were born in New York.)

FRONTISPIECE.

Arrival near Portsmouth.

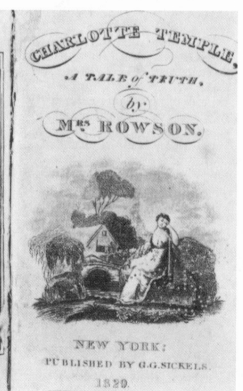

CHARLOTTE TEMPLE,
A TALE OF TRUTH,
by
Mr ROWSON.

NEW YORK:
PUBLISHED BY G.G.SICKELS.
1829.

Captain (later Colonel) John Montrésor, depicted in a portrait possessed by his descendants.

In 1774, the year that Montrésor supposedly seduced Charlotte, and in the two following years, he was—according to his diaries—in Boston as the engineer in charge of British fortifications.

Whether or not Montrésor was the guilty man, was there a Charlotte Stanley? There were two Charlottes in the Derby family at the time of the novel's publication, but neither fits Mrs. Rowson's description of her tragic anti-heroine. Neither Mrs. Rowson's Charlotte nor her father appears in British reference books dealing with the nobility, but Charlotte—if she ever lived— could have been excluded because of her blemished virtue. And her father—if he ever lived—may have been ignored because he married beneath his station and had been disinherited.

Yet there is the grave in Trinity Churchyard and there is a tombstone above it. A lengthy commentary in the Funk & Wagnalls definitive 1905 edition of *Charlotte: A Tale of Truth* explains their presence thus: Charlotte's daughter, Lucy, grown up, came to America to find her mother's grave. Though it was unmarked, Tommy Collister, a longtime Trinity sexton (for whom Collister Street in Manhattan is named), immediately led Lucy to the place. Lucy had her mother's bones exhumed and taken to England, and placed a tombstone over the vacant grave, affixing to the stone a silver plate engraved *To the Memory of Charlotte Stanley, age 19.* The plate subsequently was stolen, but it was retrieved; it then remained on the tombstone until the construction of the present Trinity Church—the third on the site—in 1846. During the construction, an engine room for a hoist stood above the empty grave. When the job was completed and the engine room dismantled, the silver plate was missing from the stone. So William H. Crommelin, foreman of the stonecutters on the construction job, had "CHARLOTTE TEMPLE" chiseled in the brown sandstone. Why Charlotte Temple rather than Charlotte Stanley? Because, the Funk & Wagnalls commentary suggests, Crommelin decided to use the name familiar to the novel's readers.

Does the story stand up? Again, the evidence is inconclusive. The tombstone does have an indentation that appears to have accommodated a silver plate. And Crommelin did have the stone carved with Charlotte's fictional name. In a fine hand but shaky syntax, he wrote to William Kelby, Librarian of the New-York Historical Society, on July 8, 1876: "Dear Sir:

Yours of June 19 received, as to your first inquiry concerning Charlotte Temple's tombstone, while erecting the present church the engine room was over it, the rumor was that the plate had been taken away during the time that the engine remained there.

Acting then as foreman of stone cutting [I] caused simply the name to be cut in."

But Crommelin's reference to "your first inquiry" indicates that Kelby had asked other questions. Did Crommelin evade answering whether or not he had perpetrated a hoax? Had he created a

Just where Charlotte Temple lived in New York was long debated by readers of the novel, and one much-favored site was The Old Tree House, at the Bowery and Pell Street. Though The Old Tree House had vanished many years earlier, a bar in the building that replaced it called itself Old Tree House.

grave for a fictional Charlotte or had there been one before the construction job? Unlike Crommelin's letter, Kelby's apparently no longer exists, so we shall never know what, if anything, Crommelin concealed.

If Charlotte really did once lie in Trinity Churchyard, the church's records offer no evidence; the oldest surviving book documenting burials dates to May

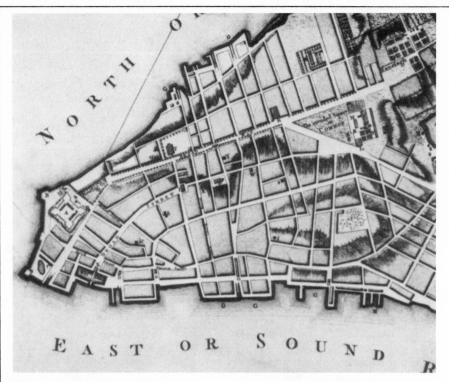

of 1777, and Charlotte, in the novel, died several years earlier.

So the mystery remains unsolved, perhaps forever.

Only one mystery surrounds Mrs. Rowson, Charlotte's creator or biographer, who might herself have been a Jane Austen heroine. Susanna Haswell before her marriage, she was born in England in 1761 but her father, a Royal Navy lieutenant, brought her to America when she was eight; he had been assigned to New England and acquired an estate at Nantasket. Young Susanna quickly impressed a neighbor, the patriot James Otis, by her knowledge of the Greek and Latin classics and her familiarity with English literature. "My little scholar," Otis called her.

When the Revolution erupted, Haswell was imprisoned and his estate confiscated; exchanged after two-and-a-half years, he returned broke to England. There Susanna took a job as a governess in the household of the Duchess of Devonshire, and in her spare time wrote a novel, *Victoria* which was published in 1786. Its purchasers included General John Burgoyne and New England's own Sam Adams, and the book proved so successful that it won Susanna an introduction to the Prince of Wales (later George IV), from whom she wangled a pension for her father. The same year she married William Rowson, a trumpeter in the Royal Horse Guards, and when a private business venture of Rowson's failed, she took to the stage with her husband and his sister.

After touring England and Scotland, Susanna appeared in Philadelphia, Boston, Baltimore, and Annapolis for three years, beginning in 1793; offstage, she churned out plays. With the success of *Charlotte: A Tale of Truth*, she quit the stage in 1796, settled in the New England in which she had spent her childhood, and opened a fashionable girls' school. In the twenty-five years that she spent as an educator—the rest of her life—she also edited a magazine, wrote more novels, verse, and a popular song, translated Homer and Virgil, and compiled *A Spelling Dictionary*. She died in Boston on November 2, 1824, and, like Charlotte, she does not rest beneath her own tombstone. She was buried inside Boston's St. Michael's Church, but the stone on which her name is engraved, along with the names of two kinsmen, is in the churchyard.

The only mystery attached to her is this: would she—a woman of character and high intelligence—have lied about Charlotte and Montrésor? And if she lied, why?

The Other Hamilton Grave

The best-known grave in Trinity Churchyard is Alexander Hamilton's, forty feet from Broadway and ten from the iron fence on Rector Street. Forgotten, nearby, lies Philip Hamilton, the statesman's eldest son; he died in 1801, three years before his father, in a duel with a young attorney named George L. Eacker, with whom he had quarreled over politics. Eacker, who died the same year that Aaron Burr killed the elder Hamilton, was buried in St. Paul's Churchyard.

The Oldest Mark of the White Man

The most venerable imprint of European settlement on Manhattan's soil is a grave in Trinity Churchyard that is older than Trinity itself. It was part of a public cemetery established in 1662 and deeded to Trinity when the church was founded in 1697. The

Painted about 1846, when the present Trinity Church had just been completed, a watercolor by Mrs. W. A. Palmer shows the historic graveyard cluttered with shacks used by the construction crews.

grave is a child's, and the sandstone slab that marks it is inscribed:

> W.C.
> HEAR . LYES . THE . BODY
> OF . RICHARD . CHURCH
> ER . SON . OF . WILLIA
> M. CHURCHER . WHO .
> DIED . THE . 5 . OF . APRIL
> 1681 . OF . AGE 5 YEARS
> AND . 5 . MONTHS

Close by, another stone records the death of Anne Churcher, age seventeen, on May 16, 1791. Her relationship to little Richard is unknown.

The Jewish Graveyards

Except for little Richard Churcher's grave in Trinity Churchyard, the oldest relic of Manhattan's early settlement is the tiny Jewish burial ground at 55-57 St. James Place, just south of Chatham Square. Established in 1683 by what became Congregation Shearith Israel (Remnant of Israel)—the Spanish and Portuguese Synagogue on Central Park West—the 54-by-52-foot plot is the resting place of the famous Rabbi Gershom Mendez Seixas, a Providence-born Revolutionary patriot and one of the clergymen at George Washington's inauguration as President. The oldest tombstone, dated 1683, is that of Benjamin·Bueno de Mesquita.

The cemetery, which once occupied much of Chatham Square, was the site of a gun battery set up by the Revolutionary commander, Major General Charles Lee, in 1776. A tablet describes the cemetery as the congregation's first, but it is actually the second; the first Jewish settlers, who arrived in 1654, petitioned Governor Peter Stuyvesant in 1655 for a burying place, but he turned them down on the ground that they did not need one yet. The next year they were allotted an area; the location of which is now forgotten; it was probably just north of Wall Street, close to the first Christian cemetery, which was later incorporated into Trinity Churchyard. A third Shearith Israel cemetery, established in 1805, survives at 72-76 West 11th Street. Like the St. James Place Plot, it was once much larger; the cutting through of West 11th Street in 1830 reduced it to its present minuscule size.

First Jewish congregation's oldest surviving burial ground, in St. James Place, contains tombstone of one Josiah Ellis, who died in 1598.

The Marble Cemeteries

What must be the least visible graveyard in the city occupies a 400-by-100-foot area between the Bowery and Second Avenue and between Second and Third streets. Called the New York Marble Cemetery and once famous and fashionable, it is now surrounded by tenements and business establishments, and can be glimpsed by pedestrians only through an iron gate on Second Avenue and a littered alley beyond the gate. It has no tombstones; the 1,500 bodies said to be interred there, which include the remains of some of New York's best-known pre-Civil War citizens, rest in 156 underground vaults. The cemetery corporation was organized in 1830, but it had disappeared from the City Directory by 1899; in this century its affairs have been handled by a member of a Trinity Place law firm.

Almost identically named but

Iron gate on Second Avenue opens onto littered alley, which leads to the once-fashionable New York Marble Cemetery.

Casket containing remains of former President James Monroe (below) is exhumed in 1858 for transfer from the New York City Marble Cemetery on Second Street to Richmond, in Monroe's native Virginia.

much more visible, the New York City Marble Cemetery lies close by, on Second Street east of Second Avenue. There are buildings on two sides and a high brick wall on a third, but it can be seen through a handsome iron fence on Second Street. It was established in 1831, a year after its neighbor, and contains 256 vaults in its 375-by-110-foot lot.

One vault once sheltered the body of former President James Monroe, who moved to New York in 1830 and died July 4, 1831, just as the cemetery opened. Interred with military pomp that enhanced the cemetery's prestige, the body lay there until the Virginia legislature in 1857 requested it for Monroe's native state. While church bells tolled and every ship in the harbor flew its flag at half-mast, the body was exhumed on July 2, 1858, to lie in state at the Church of the Annunciation on 14th Street. Then, escorted by the Seventh Regiment, the body was sent by steamer to Richmond.

The body of John Ericsson,

builder of the ironclad Civil War battleship *Monitor*, rested in the cemetery until 1890, when it was returned to Sweden. Still interred there are Thomas A. Emmet, physician, lawyer, state attorney general and an organizer of the city's first railway, who was an exile from Ireland, and a brother

of the Irish patriot Robert Emmet; James Lenox, whose Lenox Library is incorporated in the New York Public Library at 42nd Street and for whom Lenox Avenue is named; Mayors Stephen Allen, Isaac Varian, and Marinus Willett, the Revolutionary War radical and colonel for whom Willett Street is named; six Roosevelts, including James Henry Roosevelt, founder of Roosevelt Hospital; the Kip family of Kips Bay; Moses Taylor, who financed Cyrus Field's first Atlantic cable; and John Lloyd Stephens, who pioneered in Mayan archaeological research in Mexico and whose vault bears a Mayan glyph. According to tradition in New York, those of early Dutch clergymen who died in the city lie in the Ministers' Vault; they supposedly were moved there from the old Dutch church that was destroyed in the great fire of 1835. Though most of the vaults are no longer used—and forgotten or ownerless, because families have died out—an interment in the cemetery took place as recently as July of 1975. The cemetery is maintained by a small endowment originated by James Maitland, grandnephew of James Lenox, and by contributions for which the trustees appeal annually to surviving vault owners. The Landmarks Preservation Commission designated it a landmark on March 4, 1969.

Thomas A. Emmet (top left), James Lenox (top right) and James Henry Roosevelt (bottom left) are among the once-famous New Yorkers whose remains lie in the New York City Marble Cemetery.

The Jumel Mansion "Ghosts"

The least wraithlike ghosts in town—if ghosts they are—have been sighted at the Jumel Mansion at 160th Street and Edgecombe Avenue. Solid-looking apparitions splendidly garbed in the fashion of the elegant old house's historic heyday, they moved about vigorously in morning sunlight; the skeptical might well dismiss them as pranksters or actors enhancing the mood of the place. But they are not so easily explicable, to wit:

1) A class of schoolgirls and their woman teacher were waiting outside for the museum's opening one morning in 1964, when a female figure in Colonial dress called down to them from an upper balcony to be less noisy. But the woman was not a member of the museum staff, the building's doors were locked at the time she appeared, and a subsequent search failed to turn up any further sign of her.

2) Four years later, in 1968, some junior-high-school students led by a man teacher were investi-

Haunted or not, the historic Jumel Mansion had a stark and ghostly look when it was photographed in 1892, more than half a century before visiting schoolchildren of the 1960s encountered terrifying and inexplicable figures on the balcony and in the attic.

gating the third-floor attic when a male figure in a Revolutionary War military uniform approached them, brandishing a sword. The youngsters and their teacher fled in terror. It was in the third-floor attic that Stephen Jumel, the huge, handsome Frenchman who had bought the house, died after a strange fall from a wagon; not long before, his wife, the beautiful but scandalous Betsey Bowen, had obtained title to the mansion by persuading Jumel to give her power of attorney over his affairs. A servant who supposedly witnessed Jumel's death is said to have mysteriously disappeared. Betsey later married the seventy-two-year-old Aaron Burr.

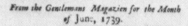

Fourteen years after its birth, Bradford's Gazette still filled its pages with "borrowed" text.

The Publisher's Problems

New York's first newspaper appeared on October 16, 1725. A weekly entitled *New York Gazette*, it was published by William Bradford (see page 24) and printed on foolscap-size, grayish, dirty-looking paper. Its news judgment was less than acute. A typical item, datelined London, March 15, 1727: "Yesterday morning died, aged eighty-five, Sir Isaac Newton, Master of His Majesty's Mint at the Tower, to which place is annexed a salary of £500 per annum, and President of the Royal Society."

Like many a newspaper publisher after him, Bradford found he was in a tough racket. The *Gazette's* issue of June 17, 1728, complained editorially: " . . . the first of May last it was two years and a half that we have continued its Publication; but having calculated the Charge of Printing and Paper for the Same, as also how much will arise to defray that Charge (when all those who take this *Gazette* have paid in what is due to the first of May last) do find that we shall loose Thirty-five pounds in the two years and a half, by Publishing this Paper, besides the trouble and charge of Correspondents, collecting the News, making up Pacquets and conveying the same to those in the Country who take them. And therefore if some further Encouragement be not given, by a larger Number of Subscribers for said *Gazette*, we must let it fall and cease Publishing the same." But Bradford kept the paper going until November 19, 1744. When Bradford quit, Henry de Forrest, who had been Bradford's apprentice and then his partner, started the *New York Evening Post*, which died in 1752, of unknown causes.

A Voice for Blacks

The first newspaper anywhere published and edited by blacks for blacks was *Freedom's Journal,* which appeared in New York on March 16, 1827. The founders were John Brown Russwurm, the first black graduate of Bowdoin College, and Samuel E. Cornish, who in 1821 had become the minister of the newly established Negro Presbyterian Church on Rose Street.

Their first editorial said, in part: "We wish to plead our own cause. Too long have others spoken for us. Too long has the public been deceived by misrepresentations in things which concern us dearly, though, in the estimation of some, mere trifles; for though there are many in society who exercise toward us benevolent feelings, still (with sorrow we confess it) there are others who make it their business to enlarge upon the least trifle which tends to the

John B. Russwurm

discredit of any person of color, and pronounce anathemas and denounce our whole body for the misconduct of this guilty one. We are aware that there are many instances of vice among us, but we avow that it is because no one has taught its subjects to be virtuous; many instances of poverty, because no sufficient efforts accommodated to minds contracted by slavery and deprived of early education have been made, to

teach them how to husband their hard earnings and to assure to themselves comforts. Education being an object of the highest importance to the welfare of society, we shall urge upon our brethren the necessity and expediency of training their children, while young, to habits of industry and thus forming them for becoming useful members of society."

The paper expired on March 28, 1829, and its last editorial read: "We consider it mere waste of words to talk of ever enjoying citizenship in this country."

Russworm then moved to Liberia.

The Rev. Samuel E. Cornish and part of the front page of the first issue of Freedom's Journal.

LANDMARKS

The First City Hall

The first City Hall in Manhattan began its career as a tavern and the town's first hotel. Governor Willem Kieft had it built at 71-73 Pearl Street in 1642 when he tired of entertaining visitors and traveling traders at home. A fifty-foot-square stone building with walls three stories high and two more stories under a pitched roof, it was leased out by the city as the *Stadt Herberg* (City Tavern), but officials conducted their business on the upper floors, within easy

Drawn in 1679 by a Dutch tourist, picture of the first City Hall shows building's walls rising four stories, below a dormered attic, and places structure well back from river. Written accounts and other drawings depict it as in the text above.

reach of bar service. Twelve years later, when the town called Fort Amsterdam was granted municipal government and became New Amsterdam, the edifice was made the *Stadt-Huys* (City Hall). The East River lapped at its foundations—Pearl Street was on the waterfront then—and over the decades the structure fell into such disrepair that in 1697 jurors refused to meet in it for fear it would fall in on them. The city sold it on August 23, 1699, for £920 to a merchant named John Rodman; he got no bargain, for the building soon had to be torn down. But parts of the original foundation and walls survived in its successor until the 1960s. After years as a parking lot, the site is to be occupied by an office building, which was under construction in 1980.

The Oldest Schoolhouse

The city's—and the nation's—oldest little red schoolhouse, built in 1696, survives at Arthur Kill Road, between Center Street and Clarke Avenue, in Staten Island's Richmondtown, a miniature version of Virginia's Williamsburg. The building is called the Voorlezer House, because the teacher,

The Voorlezer House

who lived there, was a *voorlezer,* a layman who conducted Dutch Reformed Church services within it in the absence of an ordained clergyman. As a school, the building was superseded in 1701 by a new church in Port Richmond. The Staten Island Historical Society, which restored and maintains the Voorlezer House, dismisses the claim of a St. Augustine, Florida, school building to be older.

Richmond Hill—They All Slept There

The city's most glamorous house, in which Lord Jeffrey Amherst, General George Washington, and Vice-Presidents John Adams and Aaron Burr once dwelt and in which Thomas Jefferson and "Baron" Frederick William Augustus Henry Ferdinand von Steuben dined splendidly with ambassadors, looked down on the Hudson from a great garden on a hilltop at what is now Charlton and Varick streets. Called Richmond Hill, it took its name from the southwesternmost, 100-foot peak of a miniature range known as the Zantberg (Sandhill). "From the crest of this small eminence," a contemporary wrote of the house, "was an enticing prospect: on the south, the woods and dells and winding road from the lands of Lispenard, through the valley where was Borrowson's tavern; and on the north and west the plains of Greenwich Village made up a rich prospect to gaze on."

Abraham Mortier, who had prospered by providing supplies to British troops well before the Revolution, bought the land in 1760 and built as his home "a wooden building of massive architecture, with a lofty portico supported by Ionic columns, the front walls decorated with pilasters of the same order, and its whole appearance distinguished by a Palladian character of rich though sober ornament." Mortier quickly made the house renowned for its hospitality, and Sir Jeffrey Amherst (not yet a lord) used it as his headquarters after winning the French and Indian War. Washington occupied it as *his* headquarters in 1776 and Aaron Burr, as a youthful aide-de-camp to Washington, fell in love with the place and determined to live in it. But John Adams beat Burr to it, taking it as his official mansion after he had been elected Vice President. A chronicler of the time described an Adams dinner party there:

"In the center of the table sat Vice-President Adams in full dress, with his bag and *solitaire*, his hair frizzled out each side of his face as you see it in Stuart's older pictures of him. On his right sat Baron Steuben, our royalist republican disciplinarian general. On his left was Mr. Jefferson, who had just returned from France, conspicuous in his red waist-coat and breeches, the fashion of Versailles. Opposite sat Mrs. Adams, with her cheerful, intelligent face. She was placed between the Count du Moustiers, the French ambassador, in his red-heeled shoes and ear-rings, and the grave, polite and formally bowing Mr. Van Birket, the learned and able envoy of Holland. There, too, was Chancellor

Richmond Hill was the official residence of Vice President John Adams when this engraving of it was first published in 1790.

Aaron Burr in 1809

Livingstone, then still in the prime of his life, so deaf as to make conversation with him difficult, yet so overflowing with wit, eloquence, and information that while listening to him the difficulty was forgotten. The rest were members of Congress, and of our Legislature, some of them no inconsiderable men."

When Adams became President, in 1797, Aaron Burr at last moved into Richmond Hill. He took a sixty-nine-year lease on the house on May 1, 1797, and lived in it before and during his vice-presidency. He entertained Jerome Bonaparte and Talleyrand there, and it was from there that he went on a July dawn in 1804 to his duel with Alexander Hamilton, which ended his political career. He gave up the house in 1807.

Richmond Hill had a few more years of glory, as the home of a world-traveled lawyer, but in 1817 the City Planning Commissioners razed the Zantberg and cut away the land beneath the house, lowering the building to the level of the new streets they had opened. Richmond Hill was a tavern for a while, and then became a disreputable theater; it was demolished in 1849.

Fraunces Tavern—Monument to Black Enterprise

Often accepted as the oldest surviving building in Manhattan, the present Fraunces Tavern actually incorporates only a few segments of the original. But even if the present structure did not exist, its site would merit a sizable bronze tablet. A decade before the first settlers arrived, history was being made on the spot: it was there in 1614 that Captain Adriaen Block built the sixteen-ton yacht *Onrust* (Restless) in which he explored Long Island Sound and sailed around the island that bears his name (see page 36).

The site's first building was an elegant house erected in 1719 by Etienne (Stephen) de Lancey, a Huguenot from Caen who had come to Manhattan in 1686 and used his mother's jewels to go into business. The £300-lot for the house was a gift from Colonel Stephanus Van Cortlandt, father of De Lancey's wife, Anne.

(Stephanus and his brother Jacobus both served as mayor of the city, and the De Lanceys' daughter Susannah married Admiral Sir Peter Warren.) After the De Lanceys moved to Broadway in 1730, they leased their old home to a dancing master, Henry Holt, who made it the scene of glittering balls.

Eventually, the building became a warehouse for De Lancey, Robinson & Co., importers of European and East India goods. Samuel Fraunces bought it for a tavern in 1762. A West Indian black man who originally spelled his surname Francis, Fraunces had been catering to gourmets as proprietor of the Masons' Arms on Broadway. He called his new establishment the Sign of Queen Charlotte, changed it to Sign of the Queen's Head, and in 1770, as Americans became disenchanted with royalty, to Fraunces Tavern. As much for Fraunces's personality as for his skill in the kitchen and his knowledge of wines, his tavern became the

Fraunces Tavern in 1777 had changed in appearance since its days as the DeLancey home and warehouse.

Fraunces Tavern today.

city's major rendezvous: citizens convened there to denounce the Stamp Act and it was there that the Sons of Liberty met to plot New York's own 1774 Tea Party.

When Fraunces first got to know George Washington is unrecorded but in 1776 Fraunces's young and pretty daughter Phoebe became Washington's housekeeper in New York and supposedly saved the general's life (see page 26). Fraunces himself served as a private in the Revolutionary army, and though blacks usually got little notice in military records, Fraunces shows up on the rolls of the First Regiment of New York State Troops. Taken prisoner by the British, Fraunces cooked for an English general—and pilfered food for hungry fellow prisoners. In his absence from the tavern, his wife and children ran the place, entertaining British officers and presumably picking up information with every round of drinks.

Whatever Fraunces and his family actually did, it impressed Congress, which voted Fraunces its thanks and £200 "in consequence of his generous advances and kindness to American prisoners and secret services." The New York State legislature similarly honored him. When Washington and Sir Guy Carleton met at Tappan in May, 1783, to discuss peace terms, Washington had Fraunces provide their dinner, and when Washington said farewell to his officers on December 4, 1783, he chose Fraunces Tavern for the occasion. The general wrote to Fraunces: "You have invariably through the most trying times maintained a constant friendship and attention to the cause of our Country and its Independence and Freedom."

Fraunces sold the tavern in 1789 to become steward of Washington's presidential household, and when the nation's capital was moved from New York to Philadelphia, Washington took Fraunces and his whole family along. Fraunces remained the President's steward until June 9, 1794; he died the following year. Re-created, Fraunces Tavern stands as his monument.

Tavern's dining rooms maintain a Colonial ambiance

The Vanished Executive Mansion

The country's first Executive Mansion, George Washington's residence just after he had been sworn in as President, stood at No. 3 Cherry Street, where Cherry Street met Franklin Square (then called St. George Square). The house had been built in 1770 by Walter Franklin, an importer, and Washington occupied it from April 23, 1789, to February 23, 1790. The residence was demolished in 1856, and a pillar of the Brooklyn Bridge now covers the site.

George Washington did sleep there, many a night, when Walter Franklin's mansion at No. 3 Cherry Street (above) was the official presidential residence. Masonry of the Brooklyn Bridge (below) now occupies the site.

George Washington's—and Major Andre's—Church

The only surviving pre-Revolutionary public building in Manhattan is St. Paul's Chapel, at Broadway and Fulton Street. (Trinity Church is the third structure of that name on its site, and Fraunces Tavern is largely a reconstruction.) Built in 1766 of stone from the land on which it stands, St. Paul's acquired its tower and steeple in 1796; otherwise it has been little altered. It is styled after London's St. Martin-in-the-Fields, because its architect, Thomas McBean, studied under St. Martin's designer, James Gibbs, a pupil of Sir Christopher Wren. When British troops occupied New York during the Revolution, worshippers at St. Paul's included Lord Howe, Sir Guy Carleton, the luckless Major John Andre, and a youthful midshipman who in 1830 became King William IV of England. George Washington and his Cabinet prayed in St. Paul's immediately after Washington took the oath of office as President on April 30, 1789, and Washington worshipped there regularly before the nation's capital was moved to Philadelphia in 1790.

In this 1899 view from the southwest, St. Paul's serenely holds its own against the precursors of modern skyscrapers. The twin-towered structure in left background was the Park Row Building. The old Central Post Office and the Astor House, an elegant hostelry, both long since demolished, stood at left.

John Adams

John Adams' White House in the Bronx

The only surviving Executive Mansion in the city is the pre-Revolutionary Vincent-Halsey House, at 3701 Provost Avenue in the Bronx's Eastchester section. From it, President John Adams conducted the nation's business for several months while a yellow-fever epidemic raged in Philadelphia, then the country's capital. Adams chose the house as his refuge because his daughter Abigail and her husband, Colonel William Smith, were living in it. On the morning after his arrival there, Adams wrote:

> "East Chester, 12th of October, 1797

To T. Pickering, Sec. of State. Dear Sir: I arrived here last night with my family and I shall make this house my home until we can go to Philadelphia with safety. If you address your letters to me at East Chester and recommend them to the care of my son, Charles Adams, Esq., at New York, I shall get them without much loss of time, but if a mail could be made up for East Chester, they might come sooner.

> With great regards, etc.
> John Adams"

The house, alas, does not have official landmark status.

Once the Executive Mansion, the Vincent-Halsey House in the Bronx displays no hint of its past glamor.

Mr. Mooney's Thriving Old Town House

The oldest surviving town house in Manhattan is a three-story Colonial Georgian structure at 18 Bowery, on the corner of Pell Street, in the heart of Chinatown. It was built between 1785 and 1789 by Edward Mooney, a wholesale butcher, on property that he acquired after it had been confiscated from James de Lancey,* who fought for the British during the Revolution. Mooney kept a racing stable there and—to what no doubt would have been his delight—the building's ground floor is now occupied by the city's busiest OTB office, which takes bets in Chinese. (Upper-floor tenants include *Pei Mei* (North American) *News*, a Chinese newspaper; the Council of Asian-American Women; an investment firm; and an acupuncturist.) Two bronze plaques, one in English and one in Chinese, recount the building's history; the one in Chinese is the first in a foreign tongue on any New York landmark. The building's owners, Mr. and Mrs. Norman Lau Kee and Mr. and Mrs. Chin Po Liu, preserve it lovingly: when a cellar door needed to be replaced, they paid $100 for handwrought nails, in keeping with the character of

De Lancey was the grandson of Etienne (Stephen) de Lancey, founder of the family in America, and the nephew of the James de Lancey who became a New York Supreme Court judge at the age of twenty-eight. During the Revolution, De Lancey headed a band of fifty mounted pro-British guerrillas known as De Lancey's Horse, who terrorized Westchester; they were nicknamed "The Cowboys" because of their raids on cattle. At the Revolution's end, De Lancey moved to Nova Scotia, where he became prominent in government.

Still elegant despite the Off-Track Betting Office that occupies the ground floor, the Mooney House has dozens of Chinese shops and offices for its neighbors. Automobile traffic clogs the Bowery where Mooney's stableboys once exercised his race horses.

the building. (Mr. Kee, a native New Yorker who holds a B.S. in mechanical engineering from M.I.T. and a J.D. from Fordham Law School, is an attorney. Mr. Liu, who earned master's degrees in public administration and business management at the University of Missouri, is a native of Kwantung and the biggest producer of bean sprouts east of Chicago.) Neither the Kees nor the Lius bet on racehorses.

Castle Clinton—Born Again

The landmark with the most varied career is Castle Clinton National Monument in Battery Park. Originally named West Battery, it was built in 1807 as a fort, although almost everyone but the army engineers knew that the best place to discourage an invading fleet was the Narrows, at the entrance to the Upper Bay. (The engineers were headed by Colonel Jonathan Williams, for whom Castle Williams on Governors Island was named.) The fort stood on a pile of rocks offshore and was connected to the mainland by a bridge, a popular spot for fishermen until the intervening water was filled in, just before the Civil War. The fort was renamed Castle Clinton in 1815, in honor of Mayor De Witt Clinton, and turned over to the city in 1822, after which it was remodeled into a kind of Madison Square Garden, and called Castle Garden. The Marquis de Lafayette was welcomed there when he came to town in 1824 for a final, emo-

Lafayette's arrival on August 16, 1824, (above) crowded the waters surrounding Castle Garden with small boats, sailing ships and even a steamboat. By 1852 Castle Garden (right) looked less like the fort it had been and more like the theater it had become.

Jenny Lind's first appearance in America, on September 11, 1850, packed Castle Garden (above) to the top balcony and proved a triumph for the entrepreneur, P. T. Barnum. In its days as the New York Aquarium (above, right), the building provided a quite different kind of entertainment to a steady stream of visitors.

After having virtually disappeared, the historic structure has been re-created (below) in its original form: once again it is Castle Clinton.

tional visit; Professor Samuel Finley Breese Morse demonstrated the basic principles of the electric telegraph there in 1835; and P. T. Barnum presented the singer Jenny Lind there in her American debut in 1850. Between 1855 and 1890 the former fort served as a reception center for immigrants, and before it was replaced by Ellis Island more than seven and a half million newcomers passed through its doors. Between 1896 and 1941,

the building housed the New York Aquarium, where thousands of financial district workers used to spend pleasant lunch hours. The Aquarium was torn down to make way for the Brooklyn-Battery tunnel. When only the shell of the building remained, Castle Clinton became a national monument in 1946. It has supposedly been restored to a reasonable facsimile of its original appearance.

The Last Fire Tower

The city's only surviving fire tower, from which firemen were to keep watch for trouble, stands in Harlem's Marcus Garvey Park, formerly Mount Morris Park. Built in 1857, the tower was designed by James Bogardus, who also designed the first cast-iron textile warehouses downtown. Bogardus descended from the Reverend Everardus Bogardus, Fort Amsterdam's second clergyman.

Typical of Bogardus's fire towers, this one was built in 1851 and stood at 33rd Street and Ninth Avenue. The drawing was made in 1852.

The sculpture that shocked people during the Gay Nineties.

The Naked Diana

The first sculpture anywhere in America of an unclad female outraged lots of New Yorkers in 1890 when it was placed atop Stanford White's Madison Square Garden, which overlooked Madison Square from the site of the New York Life Insurance Company building at 51 Madison Avenue. The figure, executed by Augustus Saint-Gaudens, represented the goddess Diana, and it survived the uproar because J. P. Morgan, the Garden's major stockholder, did not shock easily.

The Smallest Plot?

What may be the smallest chunk of real estate on Manhattan is a triangle in the sidewalk on Seventh Avenue South between Waverly Place and Perry Street. Designated Block 12, Lot 46, it measures one foot three inches, two feet one and a half inches, and one foot nine and an eighth inches. In recent years it has been assessed at $100 and has cost $6.90 in taxes.

The Narrowest House

The city's narrowest house stands at 75½ Bedford Street, in Greenwich Village; it is nine and a half feet wide, thirty feet long, and three stories high. Edna St. Vincent Millay and John Barrymore lived there—at different times.

"For Sale" sign covers a good one-third of the facade of 75½ Bedford Street, which as a half-size house, has to make do with half a house number.

Washington Square Memorial Arch

The Washington Square Memorial Arch, which has towered over the southern end of Fifth Avenue since 1889, was first constructed of wood and then was re-created in marble by popular demand. The idea for the arch originated with William Rhinelander Stewart, who lived at 17 Washington Square North: when he read in the newspapers that there would be a parade on April 30 to commemorate George Washington's inauguration as President a hundred years earlier and that the parade would proceed along the square and up Fifth Avenue, he decided that the parade must have an arch through which to march. A prominent citizen, Stewart solicited contributions from residents of the square, Waverly Place and Fifth Avenue up to 14th Street, but rejected them from outlanders who lived beyond those precincts. He raised $2,765, and the architect Stanford White donated the design. White's wooden structure, of delicate and elegant Colonial proportions, was topped by a ten-foot wooden statue of Washington, which had stood at the Battery in 1792. The whole thing cost $66.50 less than Stewart had collected. The arch was so widely acclaimed that within a week of its debut a committee headed by Stewart was formed to perpetuate it in marble. Stanford White again provided the design, and this time contributions were accepted from anyone: a benefit recital at the old Metropolitan Opera House by Ignace Jan Paderewski raised $4,500, and the workmen who cut the marble at the Tuckahoe Quarry chipped in (oops!) $100. The completed arch, 73 feet 6 inches high overall and 47 feet 9 inches high at its opening, exceeded its $150,000 budget by $28,000. It was dedicated on April 30, 1895. The group sculpture on the western pedestal, with George Washington as its central figure, was added in 1918; it was executed by Alexander Stirling Calder, the father of Alexander Calder.

Wooden version of the Washington Arch, beflagged and beribboned, awaits its first parade in 1889 (left). Half a century later (opposite page) the crack 82nd Airborne Division marches under the wooden arch's marble successor in celebration of the victory the division helped to win in World War II.

The Instant Hotel

The fastest-built structure ever put up on Manhattan was a three-hundred-guest hotel erected in Greenwich Village in a single weekend in 1822 to shelter refugees from a yellow-fever epidemic in the city proper. A historian of the time wrote that "the Rev'd Mr. Marselus . . . informed me that he saw corn growing on the present corner of Hammond [West 11th] and Fourth Streets on a Saturday morning, and on the following Monday Sykes & Niblo had a house erected capable of accommodating three hundred boarders."

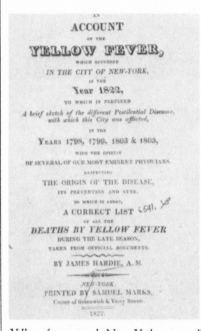

Yellow fever struck New York repeatedly in the late 18th and early 19th centuries and a book published in 1822 listed the victims for the information of survivors.

The Church's Best Buy

The biggest real estate bargain since the purchase of Manhattan from the Indians involved the sale of the site of St. Patrick's Cathedral: the city turned it over to the church in 1857 for $1.

St. Patrick's Cathedral

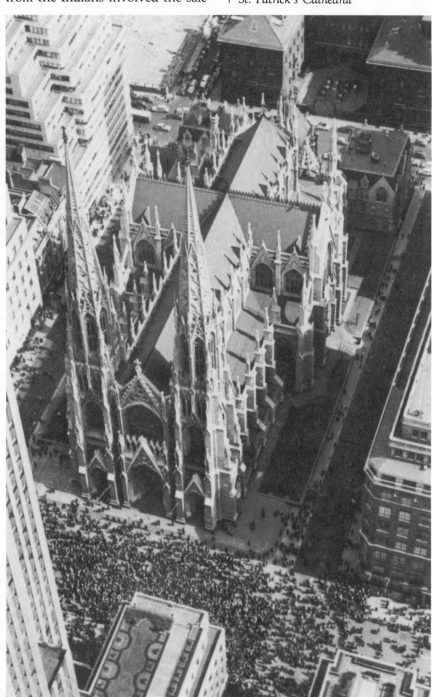

Outerbridge-The Bridge Far Out

The city's farthest out bridge, and a bustling landmark, is the Outerbridge Crossing connecting Tottenville, Staten Island, and Perth Amboy, New Jersey, across the Arthur Kill—but its location did not give it its name. The span commemorates Eugenius H. Outerbridge, a Staten Islander in the import-export business and the first chairman of the Port Authority, which built the bridge. The Outerbridge Crossing and the Goethals Bridge—which links Elizabeth, New Jersey, and Howland Hook, Staten Island, over the Arthur Kill—were the Port Authority's first ventures: both were opened to traffic on June 29, 1928, nine days after their dedication. (The dedication ceremonies had been put ahead of schedule so that Governor Alfred E. Smith could attend, for on opening day Smith was in Houston, Texas, where he had just been chosen as the Democratic nominee for the presidency.) The Goethals Bridge was named for Major General George W. Goethals, chief engineer of the Panama Canal and the Port Authority's first consulting engineer. By coincidence, opening day was Goethal's seventieth birthday—but the general had died several months earlier, unaware of the honor to be bestowed on him.

A month before it was opened to traffic, Outerbridge Crossing (top) appeared to be a long way from completion. The Outerbridge and the Goethals Bridge were dedicated on the same day, June 20, 1928; In photograph at right, Governor Alfred E. Smith, who was about to become the Democratic candidate for the presidency, is shown speaking at the Goethals Bridge ceremonies.

HOLIDAYS

The First St. Patrick's Day

The first recorded observance of St. Patrick's Day in New York occurred in 1762. The *New York Mercury* of March 15, 1762, announced: "The Anniversary Feast of St. Patrick is to be celebrated on Wednesday the 17th Instant, at the house of Mr. John Marshall, at Mount Pleasant, near the College; Gentlemen that please to attend will meet with the best Usage." Neither the *Mercury* nor any other newspaper covered the event, but in 1776 the *New York Gazette* of March 20 and the *Mercury* of March 24 reported identically:

"Monday last being the Day of St. Patrick, tutelar Saint of Ireland, was ushered in at the Dawn, with Fifes and Drums, which produced a very agreeable Harmony before the Doors of many Gentlemen of that Nation, and others.

"Many of them assembled and

St. Patrick's Day parade in 1874: the scene is Union Square and the artist who recorded it was looking toward Broadway.

spent a joyous tho' orderly Evening, at the House of Mr. Bardin in this City, where the following Healths were drank, Viz.

"1. The King and Royal House of Hanover.
"2. The Governor and Council of the Province.
"3. The glorious memory of King William, &c.
"4. The Memory of the late Duke of Cumberland.
"5. The Day; and Prosperity to Ireland.
"6. Success to the Sons of Liberty in America, may they never want Money, Interest nor Courage to Maintain their Just Rights.

"7. Mr. Pitt.

"8. General Conway.

"9. May the Enemies of America be branded with Infamy and Disdain.

"10. May the honest Heart never know Distress.

"11. The Protestant Interest.

"12. May all Acts of Parliament, Contrary to the American Interest be laid aside.

"13. Success to American Manufacturers.

"14. May the true Sons of Liberty never want Roast Beef nor Claret.

"15. More Friends and less need.

"16. Conquest to the Lover and Honour to the Brave.

"17. May we never want Courage when we come to the Trial.

"18. The Lord Lieutenant of Ireland.

"19. May the Enemies of Ireland never eat the Bread nor drink the Whisky of it, but be tormented with Itching without the benefit of Scratching."

The reporter did not record what drinks were imbibed.

The first St. Patrick's Day parade, held on March 17, 1779, was made up entirely of "Volunteers of Ireland," recruited here by Francis, Lord Rawdon, to fight for the King. (Since the British were occupying New York, Irishmen on the side of the patriots could not celebrate in the city.) James Rivington's *Royal Gazette* of March 20 and the *New York Gazette* of March 22 described the occasion:

"Last Wednesday, the Anniversary of Saint Patrick, the Tutelar Saint of Ireland, was celebrated by the Natives of that Kingdom with their accustomed Hilarity. The Volunteers of Ireland, pre-ceded by their Band of Music, marched into the City, and formed before the House of their Colonel, Lord Rawdon, who put himself at their Head, and after paying his Compliments to his excellency General Knyphausen [a Hessian commanding the King's forces in the absence of Sir Henry Clinton] and to General Jones, accompanied them to the Bowery, where a Dinner was provided, consisting of five hundred Covers. . . ."

The first St. Patrick's Day dinner of the Society of the Friendly Sons of St. Patrick took place in 1784, the year that the Society was organized by, Society tradition has it, Irish officers of the Revolutionary Army. The dinner was served at Cape's Tavern, at 115 Broadway; the guests included the governor of New York State, and "the day and the evening," said the *New York Packet and Advertiser* on March 18, "were spent in festivity and mirth."

The First Fifth Avenue Parade

The first parade on Fifth Avenue, which was opened to traffic as far north as 13th Street in November, 1824, took place in 1830. It celebrated the 1830 revolution in France, and mounted Frenchmen wearing the uniform of their country's National Horse Guard led the long procession downtown to Washington Square. Among the thousands of participants was former President James Monroe.

Among the greatest of Fifth Avenue parades in this century was the triumphal procession of John Glenn, the astronaut, on March 1, 1962.

The First Columbus Day

The city first celebrated Columbus Day on October 12, 1792—the three-hundredth anniversary of the explorer's landing in the New World—with a banquet sponsored by the then newly organized Society of St. Tammany, or Columbian Order. But thereafter, the day went unmarked for another century, until the Columbus Monument was unveiled in 1892 in what is now Columbus Circle. When October 12 became a legal holiday in 1909, by act of the state legislature, the Italian government was so pleased that it dispatched two cruisers to New York Harbor to participate in that year's observance.

A crane lifts sculpture representing Columbus to the top of the column on October 9, 1892 (below); column and statue (right) dominate the circle today.

The First George Washington's Birthday Party

The city's first Washington's Birthday celebration took place on February 22, 1797, when Washington was sixty-five. The Battery's guns boomed. A ball was held "at the new spacious and elegant Assembly-Room in the Tontine City Tavern, Broadway." A dinner that, the *New-York Journal* said, "for taste and elegance has never been surpassed, if ever equalled in this city," was given at Delacroix's new restaurant at 112 Broadway, and the guests filled five large rooms.

But not everybody cheered. One newspaper commented acidly that the birthday had been "noticed" only by those "who are attached to the ancient Colony system of servility and adulation."

One admirer who observed the birthday annually thereafter was Mary Simpson, a black woman who had been freed from slavery by Washington and who became known as Mary Washington. For thirty years after her liberation, she sold fruits, vegetables, butter, eggs, milk, and home-baked pastries from the basement of her house at 79 John Street, between Gold and Nassau streets. Every February 22 until she died in

Overlooking Broadway and close to St. Paul's, the Tontine City Tavern was a popular meeting place for businessmen and a fashionable spot for celebrations. A ball was given there in observance of George Washington's 65th birthday.

1837, she set out a gigantic birthday cake, great quantities of punch, and large pots of hot coffee for all comers—who came in droves. Adorning the table were a leather trunk on which the initials "G. W." were studded in brass, and a large portrait of Washington—both of them gifts from the general. She explained she was afraid that if she "did not keep up the day, Washington would soon be forgotten."

Lincoln's Centennial

The city's most memorable observance of Abraham Lincoln's birthday occurred on February 12, 1909, the centennial of his birth. A million New Yorkers participated in ceremonies all over the city, but centering on Cooper Union, where a speech by Lincoln in 1860 had made him a strong contender for the Republican nomination to the presidency. Among the notables who spoke that day was Booker T. (for Taliaferro) Washington, ex-coal miner, ex-janitor, and founder of Tuskegee Institute, who addressed the Republican Club; he had been born a slave, and freed in childhood by the Emancipation Proclamation.

Celebration of Lincoln's Birthday was first proposed in 1891 by Lincoln's first-term Vice-President, Hannibal Hamlin; eighty-one years old at the time, Hamlin traveled to New York from his home in Maine to broach the idea at a dinner held by the Lincoln Club. In 1896 the state legislature made the day a legal holiday.

Lincoln in a detail of a Mathew Brady photograph.

The First Veterans Day

The first Veterans Day (né Armistice Day) was celebrated here twice, four days apart, in November of 1918; both times New Yorkers reveled in outbursts of delirious joy and uninhibited hilarity unmatched in the city's history. On November 7, Roy W. Howard reported from Europe to the United Press that Germany had surrendered and the World War had ended. Bells rang, whistles blew, offices, shops, and schools emptied into the streets, girls kissed strangers and strangers kissed girls, and 155 tons of ticker tape and waste paper fell in a blizzard on surging crowds. Then the Howard dispatch was denied,

Flags flew and ribbons of paper fluttered down from tall buildings as New York celebrated the first Armistice Day on November 11, 1918. Anyone in uniform was hailed as a hero, including the soldiers on the truck, who probably had not been overseas.

and the city relapsed into its wartime glumness. When the war did end, it seemed, it would be an anticlimax; the November 7 act would be a hard one to follow. But at 4:30 a.m. November 11, the bells rang and the whistles blew again and, once the people were convinced that this time it was for real, the celebration started anew—and proved even wilder than the first one.

TROUBLES AND ASPIRATIONS

So What's New?

Money troubles here began not long after the city itself did. The first currency controls had to be imposed on April 18, 1641; they were aimed at "bad wampum." Actually, it was not wampum but seawant that caused the problem. The Indians had two kinds of money: one, wampum, was white and was minted from periwinkle shells; the other, seawant, was fashioned from the purple of hardclam shells. Fragments of both kinds of shells were rounded, polished, pierced with sharp stones, and strung on animal sinews that were then woven into belts. A six-foot string of wampum was worth 4 guilders

($2), and the same length of seawant equaled 8 guilders.

Long Island Indians turned out the best seawant, and New England Indians, who knew nothing of seawant until the Dutch arrived, produced a sloppy imitation. But in compliance with Gresham's Law, that bad money drives out good money, poor-quality seawant flooded New Netherland, while the New England Indians made off with the good stuff. So the 1641 act "Regulating the Currency of Wampum"—the Dutch called both wampum and seawant by the same name—resulted. It read:

"Whereas very bad Wampum is at present circulating here, and payment is made in nothing but

rough, unpolished stuff which is brought here from other places, where it is 50 per cent cheaper than is paid out here, and the good, polished Wampum commonly called Manhattan Wampum is wholly put out of sight or exported, which tends to the express ruin and destruction of this Country; In order to provide in time therefor, We do, therefore,

Although belts woven of wampum, like the one below, served as currency in trading between Indians and whites, the belts originated among the Iroquois as reminders of historic events. This belt commemorated the unification of five Indian nations in a confederacy that white men called the League of the Iroquois.

for the public good, interdict and forbid, all persons of what state, quality or condition soever they be, to receive in payment, or to pay out, any unpolished Wampum during the next month of May except at Five for one stiver and that strung, and then after that Six beads for one stiver. [A stiver is a Dutch nickel.] Whosoever shall be found to have acted contrary hereunto, shall provisionally forfeit the Wampum which is paid out and 10 guilders for the Poor, and both payer and payee are alike liable. The well polished Wampum shall remain at its price as before, to wit, Four for one stiver, provided it be strung."

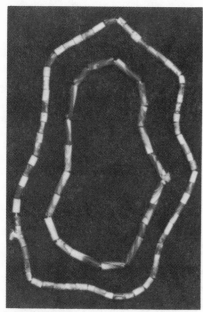

Strings of wampum like these served as currency, their value depending on the number of beads they contained.

The Idea That Is Born Again and Again

The comment in the newsweekly dealt with a suggestion that Manhattan, Staten Island, Long Island, and Westchester secede from New York State and form a new one. "The ground for the proposal is that the metropolitan ideas of the city and its suburbs clash so violently with the rural ideas of the northern part of the State that a continuance under the same government is certain to produce endless confusion, strife and conflict between the Judiciary and the Legislature. . . . It need hardly be said that the division of a State into two or more States is no new thing. Massachusetts and Virginia have both undergone the operation with manifest gain. Nor can there be any doubt but that the two States—Manhattan and Orange—that would spring out of the bi-section of New York would be well qualified to take a position among the greatest members of the confederacy. . . . The former would become a sort of Venice or Hamburg on a new and enormously increased scale." This editorial note appeared in *Harper's Weekly* for May 9, 1857. (The confederacy to which it referred was the United States, not the Confederate States, which had not yet been formed as such.) A few years later, on January 7, 1861, Mayor Fernando Wood devoted his entire inaugural address to the Common Council to an even more radical notion. "Why should not New York City, instead of supporting by her contributions in revenue two-thirds the expenses of the United States, become . . . independent? As a free city, with but a nominal duty on imports, her local government could be supported without taxation upon her people. Thus we could live free from taxes and have cheap goods nearly duty free. In this she would have the whole and united support of the Southern States as well as of all other States to whose interests and rights . . . she has always been true." Wood had more in mind than a tax haven. He was concerned, on behalf of New York bankers, that the obviously imminent Civil War might cause Southern planters to default on their $150 million in loans from the city's banks; and he hoped, on behalf of New York merchants, that the city's secession would permit them to continue to trade with the "Southern States."

THE STATE OF MANHATTAN.

A proposal has been made to divide the State of New York into two new States, drawing the line north of the Island of Manhattan, so as to include in the southern division the counties of Westchester, New York, and Richmond, with Long Island. The ground for the proposal is that the metropolitan ideas of the city and its suburbs clash so violently with the rural ideas of the northern part of the State, that a continuance under the same government is certain to produce endless confusion, strife, and conflict between the Judiciary and the Legislature. A convention is proposed to take the matter into serious consideration.

It need hardly be said that the division of a State into two or more States is no new thing. Massachusetts and Virginia have both undergone the operation with manifest gain. Nor can there be doubt but the two States—Manhattan and Orange—which would spring out of the bisection of New York, would be well qualified to take a position among the greatest members of the confederacy. We presume that the population of the State of Manhattan would not be less than 1,500,000, while the State of Orange might contain 2,500,000 souls. The former would become a sort of Venice or Hamburg, on a new and enormously increased scale.

The Harper's Weekly proposal for a State of Manhattan, as it appeared in 1857.

EDUCATION

The School That's Still Teaching

The city's first school, which still flourishes as the Collegiate School, at 241 West 77th Street, was established in 1638, two years after the local clergyman, Dominie Everardus Bogardus, asked the Dutch West India Company in Amsterdam for a schoolmaster to "teach and train the youth of both Dutch and blacks." The teacher the company sent was Adam Roelantsen, a thirty-two-year-old Dutchman who turned out to be both troublesome and disagreeable (see page 20). Classes met in Fort Amsterdam, presumably in the church. The Collegiate School's life has not been uninterrupted: school shut down during the Revolutionary War and did not resume until 1824, after what must have been the longest school vacation in history.

Dominie Everardus Bogardus, the city's second clergyman, inspired establishment of what is now the Collegiate School (right).

Discipline and Dr. Curtius

The first schoolteacher to protest that it was all the parents' fault did so in 1661: he was Alexander Carolus Curtius, who had been engaged as master of the Latin school in April, 1659, and who was reprimanded by the burgomasters on February 25, 1661, on the ground that he did "not keep strict discipline over the boys in his school, who fight among themselves and tear the clothes from each other's bodies, which he should prevent and punish." Curtius replied that "some people do not wish to have their children punished," and he asked for a law to back him up. Apparently, no such law was passed, for he resigned on July 21. Curtius's school was at 26 Broad Street.

The first kindergarten in the city opened about 1825 at Canal and Greene streets. Its daily activities (below, top and bottom), recorded by a contemporary artist, bore no resemblance to school life in a modern "open classroom."

The Requisites for a Schoolmaster

The first free grammar school was established in 1705, when the city's population was 5,250. Andrew Clarke was appointed its master after the city government petitioned the Bishop of London for an English-born teacher of good learning, pious life and conversation, and an even temper.

For the times, those were demanding criteria. No training schools for teachers existed and in most places in this country anyone who had completed sixth grade, could maintain classroom discipline and knew how to mend quill pens was considered qualified to teach. Most schools were church-run, and teachers' pay usually was only a third of what the minister got: as a result, a good many teachers were condemned as incompetent, cantankerous, lazy drunkards.

The plea to London coincided with the first successful effort in New York to establish a public school system: the New York Free School Society, organized in 1805, aimed to educate youngsters — chiefly the offspring of recent immigrants and of freed slaves — whose parents could not afford the tuition fees of religious or private institutions. Supported by philanthropy, the society schooled 600,000 children between 1805 and 1853, when its work was taken over by the New York City Board of Education.

The First Yeshiva

The first Jewish school in the city opened in 1731, shortly after *Shearith Israel*—the congregation that originated with the *Sephardim* who arrived and settled in 1654—completed a new temple.

CIVIL RIGHTS

The First Civil Rights Crusade

The city's first civil-rights crusade was begun in 1655 by two Jews within a year of the arrival of the first Jewish immigrants. The plaintiffs were Jacob bar Simson, a Hollander and the first Jew in town, and Asser Levy van Swellem, who Americanized his name to Asser Levy when he came here from Brazil. They sued the city when Governor Peter Stuyvesant, annoyed because the Jewish population had grown to around twenty families, barred Jews from serving in the militia and taxed all male Jews between the ages of sixteen and sixty-five the sum of $1.25 a month to "compensate" for their "exemption." Bar Simson and Levy contended that they

Civil rights instructions to Peter Stuyvesant emanated from the Dutch West India House in Amsterdam.

had as much right as anyone else to help defend the colony, but they lost the first round in court. Defiantly they stood guard duty anyway, and appealed to Amsterdam. On March 13, 1656, the Dutch West India Company direc-

tors wrote to Stuyvesant that "the Consent accorded these people to go to New Netherland and there to enjoy the same liberty their Nation enjoyed in Holland, included all Civil and Political privileges." Asser Levy later became one of New Amsterdam's and New York's most popular and influential citizens; Asser Levy Place is named for him.

The First Open Housing

The city's first open-housing fight began in 1656, when a young man named Salvador d'Andrada bought a house on Wall Street at auction in December, 1655. When it became known that d'Andrada, a recent immigrant from the West Indies, was Jewish, the sale was annulled, because Governor Peter Stuyvesant had decreed that Jews could not own property in New Amsterdam. D'Andrada and three fellow-immigrants, Jacob Cohen Henriques, Abraham de Lucena, and Joseph d'Acosta, appealed to the Dutch West India Company in Amsterdam. The company directors icily told Stuyvesant that they had heard of his decree "with displeasure," reminded him that Holland imposed no restrictions on the owning of property, and suggested that he was "punctually to obey" orders in the future. The directors were motivated, at least in part, by the fact that Jews were large stockholders in the Dutch West India Company.

The First Blacks' Property Rights

The city's first court decision legalizing slaveholding by blacks was handed down on April 14, 1719. The executors of the will of Jacob and Elizabeth Regnier had challenged the right of a free black named Fortune to keep three slaves he had inherited, but a jury in Mayor's Court ruled in favor of Fortune.

Patrolman Samuel Battle

The First Black Cop

The first black man to win a place on the New York police force was Samuel Battle, who was appointed in 1911 and rose to a lieutenancy. He later became a member of the Parole Commission.

The Woman Who Whipped Jim Crow

The first black New Yorker to beat Jim Crow—the practice of segregating the races in public—was Elizabeth Jennings, a school-teacher. She sued the Third Avenue Railroad Company in 1854 for having put her off a streetcar. Her lawyer, Chester A. Arthur, who had just been admitted to the bar and who later became President of the United States, won a $250 verdict for her. Her victory ended discrimination against blacks on the city's public-transportation system.

Chester A. Arthur

Two years after the scene was drawn in 1852, street cars like this had to abandon discrimination against blacks.

SPORTS

The Boxer Who Tutored Byron

The first great black boxer came from Staten Island, but he never fought a bout in the United States. He was Bill Richmond, a slave belonging to the Duke of Northumberland, who lived on Staten Island at the time of the Revolution. Richmond first demonstrated his pugilistic prowess when three Hessians picked a fight with him and he beat up all of them. When the British evacuated New York, the Duke took Richmond with him and sent him to school in England. Richmond became a professional boxer at the age of forty-two and bested all comers until he met the Englishman Tom Cribb—the greatest bare-knuckle battler in ring history—at Hailsham, Sussex, on October 2, 1805. Cribb beat Richmond in ninety bloody minutes. But Richmond was so highly regarded that an inn he established in England, the Horse and Dolphin, became a popular resort both for the nobility and for sporting folk, and a boxing school he ran included Lord Byron among its pupils. Richmond trained Tom Molineaux, a black who later became the American heavyweight champion. Richmond died in 1829.

Bill Richmond in an 1812 portrait.

The Great Catch

The city's first white fishermen were crewmen for the *Half Moon* whom Henry Hudson sent ashore on September 4, 1609. They cast a net from a beach—either Coney Island or Sandy Hook—and caught "ten great Mullets, of a foot and a halfe long a peace, and a Ray as great as foure men could hale into the ship."

The Series on the Air

The first World Series ever to be broadcast was that of 1921, in which the New York Giants faced the New York Yankees. Radio Station WJZ, based in Newark, gave a play-by-play account of the eight games. (The Series was scheduled for nine.) The Giants won five, the Yanks three. Some deception was necessitated by the state of the art. A studio announcer simply relayed details he received by telephone from a *Newark Star* reporter.

Youthful radio fans of 1921 work a crystal-and-cat's-whisker set to capture Morse code transmissions from afar. Boy in center, besides keeping set in tune, dictates incoming message to friend at the right, who records it.

The Babe at bat on Yankee Stadium's opening day, 1923.

The Crowd at the Stadium

The biggest crowd ever to attend a baseball game in New York jammed Yankee Stadium on opening day of its first season, April 18, 1923; there were 74,217 fans—another 25,000 were turned away. The Yankees defeated the Boston Red Sox 4-1, after Babe Ruth, with two men on base, hit a homer into the right-field bleachers. Bleacher seats cost a quarter.

The Natatorial Elephant

The first and only elephant known to have swum across New York's Lower Bay landed, so to speak, behind bars in the police lockup at New Dorp, Staten Island, charged with vagrancy. The beast, a gentle creature of unrecorded name and sex, performed the feat, a swim of five or six miles, on June 4, 1904—one of the livelier days, it turned out, in New Dorp's history—after a surreptitious start at dawn from somewhere on Coney Island. The animal supposedly was one of three that were reported to have fled a few days earlier from Luna Park, one of Coney Island's glamorous amusement centers at the time. It was first sighted in the water by two fishermen, Frank Krissler and a friend, whose involvement was recounted in *The New York Times* of June 5:

" . . . . yesterday morning about four o'clock they rowed about three quarters of a mile off the shore [of New Dorp] and dropped their hooks. Krissler and his friend, so they aver, were wondering if the fish were ever going to take the hook when suddenly across the still waters there came an unearthly sound. It had too much volume, they said, for a groan, was too loud for a bellow, and too deep for a siren.

"The weather was very thick and the fishermen could see only a short distance. The echoes of the first sound had hardly died away when a second and more powerful noise rent the air, and then the rowboat began to roll and the fishermen realized that the commotion was coming their way. In a minute or two a huge form hove in sight. It was off the port bow of the little boat and was preceded by something shaped like a big funnel, out of which was spouting high into the air great streams of water.

" 'Rhinoceros,' howled Krissler.

" 'Whale,' shrieked his friend.

"The boat was turned around in a jiffy and a minute later was skimming over the water at a rate of speed that would have made the Cornell eight look like a lot of oystermen.

"The huge Thing astern had sighted the fishermen, and when it saw that they were off at breakneck speed it, too, put on extra steam and started in hot pursuit.

"When the fishermen arrived at the beach it was right behind . . . ."

But the elephant offered no resistance when Krissler, his friend, and two fishermen on the beach lassoed its tusks and led it to the New Dorp police station, where it munched hay all day, waiting, as a cynical journalist suggested, for the Luna Park press agent to show up and bail it out. The other two elephants, which allegedly had headed for Quogue, on Long Island, never were sighted.

Gigantic replica of an elephant towers above a Coney Island roller coaster in this scene from about 1889. When the real elephant swam the Lower Bay, the Coney Island amusement parks had acquired a great deal more glamor.

TRANSPORTATION

The First Ferry—
A Day's Wait in Line

The city's first ferry, which ran between Dover and Pearl streets in Manhattan and Fulton Street in Brooklyn, began operating in 1638. Cornelis Dircksen started the enterprise, but he sold it in 1643, and thereafter service must have been chaotic, for Governor Peter Stuyvesant and the Council of New Netherland passed an ordinance on July 1, 1654, with a preamble that read:

"That very great confusion and disorder prevail more and more among the Ferrymen on both sides of the Ferry of the *Manhattans* to the serious inconvenience of the Passengers and Inhabitants of this Province, so that those under the necessity of going over, are frequently obliged to wait whole days and nights, and then again are constrained to give up their journey not without gross extortion of double and higher fare, disputes and other unmannerly practices. . . ."

The ordinance restricted ferry operation to a licensed lessee who had to maintain "a covered Shed or Lodge, to shelter them [passengers] from the rain, cold, &c.," and set fares thus:

	florins (40 cents)	stivers (2 cents)
For each wagon or cart with two horses or oxen,	2	10
For one cart or wagon with one horse,	2	
For one cart or plow,	1	
For one pig, sheep, buck, or goat,	[record unclear]	
For two, eight stivers, and what is above that, each,		3
For every man or woman, Indian or Squaw,		6
For two or more persons, each one,		3
For a child under ten years, half fare,		
For one horse or four footed horned beast,	1	10
For one hogshead of tobacco,		16
For one tun of beer,		16
For an anker with wine or liquor,		6
For a tub of butter, soap or such like,		6
For a mud [four bushels] of grain, and what exceeds that is ½ a stiver per Skeple [bushel]		4
Packages of goods and other articles, not specified herein, in proportion, as parties shall agree.		

In summer, service had to operate from 5 a.m. to 8 p.m., in winter from 7 a.m. to 5 p.m., subject to cancellation "when the Windmill hath lowered its sail in consequence of storm or otherwise." (The windmill was at the Battery and served as a small-craft warning.) Double fares prevailed after-hours, but the governor, councilmen, and peace officers on official business rode free at any time.

Scowlike ferry with a sail (just left of buildings) arrives at Brooklyn's Fulton Street wharf from Manhattan. Such flat-bottom craft were American in design and widely used on rivers. The scene here was recorded in 1717 by the Boston artist William Burgis.

The Horse-Powered Ferry and Its Steam-Powered Competitor

The first power ferries between Manhattan and Brooklyn went into service in 1814, with horses and steam competing as sources of energy. The horse-power boat had a paddle wheel in its center and horses walked a horizontal treadmill to keep it turning. On May 8 of the same year, Robert Fulton inaugurated a steam ferry, the *Nassau*, but it proved so costly to run that no boats of that type were added for another decade. Before the horse- and steam-powered boats, Manhattan-Brooklyn ferries were rowboats or pirogues, canoe-like craft that could be rowed or sailed or flat-bottom scows propellable by wind or mus-

cle. But the sixteen-year-old Cornelius Vanderbilt, founder of the family fortune, used a sailboat when he opened his Manhattan-Staten Island ferry in 1813.

By the 1830s, vessels of every variety crowded the harbor, seen here from Brooklyn Heights, but up the Hudson at least one horse-powered ferry (below) survived until 1854, when a steam vessel replaced it.

The Parachute That Failed

The first parachute ever demonstrated in New York was dropped by the French aeronaut J. P. Blanchard on March 4, 1797. "Mr. Blanchard's miniature balloon had a beautiful ascension," the *New York Gazette and General Advertiser* reported, "but the parachute did not prove sufficiently strong to let the quadrupeds down with safety, for one of them was killed." The quadrupeds were not identified. The mishap was a rare blemish on Blanchard's record. In 1785, he and the Boston physicist John Jeffries had crossed the English Channel from Dover to Calais by balloon in two hours and delivered the first international air mail. They landed almost naked, for the balloon had leaked and they had had to toss even their clothes overboard to lighten the load. Blanchard made at least one parachute jump, as well as sixty balloon ascents; one of them, in Philadelphia on January 9, 1793, was witnessed by a vast crowd that included President Washington.

Early parachute

The First Balloonist's Bust

The first manned balloon ascension in America was attempted in

Blanchard's balloon as it appeared in advertisement of his impending ascent.

New York on September 23, 1789. The aeronaut was an English showman named Joseph Deeker. After advertising for financial backers in the *New-York Journal and Weekly Register* and the *New York Advertiser,* he built and sent up a couple of trial balloons from the Battery: one, six feet in diameter, got as far as Harlem, and the other, a ten-footer, got to Flushing. Then he tried to ride a bigger one himself. The next day, September 24, the *New-York Journal and Weekly Register* reported: "The day arrived—crowds of spectators fly to the theater of action—our hero partly inflates his aerial vehicle—the upper retainer is loosed—and alas, the gas fails!—the balloon falls!—the fire communicates!—and the expectations of thousands ascend *in fumo.*"

The Little Railroad That Grew

The city's first railroad, chartered in April, 1831, still more or less serves thousands of commuters daily, though it has undergone several changes of name and no longer uses horses instead of newfangled, dangerous locomotives along part of its route. Now Metropolitan Transportation Authority's Harlem and Hudson Divisions, it started out as the New York and Harlem Railroad Company. It had taken a long time to get the railroad organized—one of its founders, Thomas A. Emmet, a physician and lawyer exiled from Ireland who became state attorney general (his brother was Robert Emmet, a martyr to the fight for Ireland's independence), had been dead for five years when the ground-breaking finally took place, at 32nd Street and Fourth Avenue (now Park Avenue South) on February 25, 1832. The line's charter provided for double track from the north side of 23rd Street to the Harlem River, with a branch westward, between 124th and 128th streets, to the Hudson. A few weeks after work began, the company won the city's permission to extend its tracks south to 14th Street, and later to Prince Street. The railroad began carrying passengers on November 14, 1832, between Prince Street and 14th Street on a route that took it along the Bowery, the old path to Peter Stuyvesant's farm. It had one coach, elegantly upholstered, and named *John Mason* in honor of the road's president, who was also the founder and president of the Chemical Bank. Two more coaches were added within a couple of weeks, to make up a train that stopped wherever would-be passengers hailed it; the fare was six cents, or half a shilling. The train was hauled by horses because the City Council deemed locomotives too dangerous for populated areas. Most of the city's 200,000 inhabitants opposed a railroad anyway, and cab-drivers tore up the tracks. (The railroad just put them back.)

To win friends and influence people the road's sponsors advertised:

THE NEW YORK AND HARLEM RAILROAD COMPANY
The cars will run upon the rails from Prince Street to 14th Street, in the Bowery, from 9 o'clock a.m. until 5 o'clock p.m. each fair day, except Sunday, for the purpose of affording evidence to the public of the expediency of using railroads within the city. A small charge will be made to defray expenses.

The company also organized a junket, of which the *Morning Courier and Enquirer* reported:

"The Harlem Railroad Company, with the Mayor, Corporation, and strangers of distinction, left the City Hall in carriages to the place of depot near Union Square, where two splendid cars made by Milne Parker, each with two horses, were in waiting. These cars were made low with broad iron wheels which fit the flanges of the railroad after an improved model from the Liverpool and Manchester cars. They resemble an omnibus, or rather several omnibuses attached to each other, padded with fine cloth and handsome glass windows, each capable of containing, outside and inside, fully forty passengers. The company was soon started and the horses trotted off in handsome style, with great ease, at the rate of about twelve miles an hour, followed by a number of private barouches and horsemen. Groups of spectators greeted the passengers of the cars with shouts and every window in the Bowery was filled. . . . The comfort and convenience of this railroad to our citizens will be

inconceivable. . . . It will make Harlem a suburb of New York."

For the railroad's promoters, the horsecar line was only a beginning: practical visionaries, they planned a steam railroad that would run from a splendid terminal at Broadway and Wall Street—just across from Trinity Church—all the way to Albany; with that they could capture the

Terminal of the New York & Harlem Railroad, shown here in 1860, stood at Madison Square, on the site where the first Madison Square Garden was to rise.

The 125th Street station (right foreground) was below street level when trains ran in an open cut. The Park Avenue scene depicted here dates to 1875.

rich passenger and freight trade monopolized by river steamboats. So they pushed their track southward, first to Centre and Chambers streets, just east of City Hall, then across Chambers Street and along Park Row (then called Chatham Street) to Broadway at the bottom of City Hall Park. But the track had barely been finished when they ran into trouble. De-

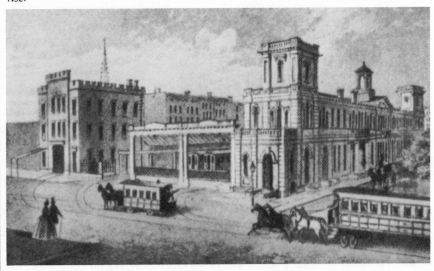

spite the ban on steam engines downtown, the railroad replaced the horses with two locomotives. The locomotives blew up, the City Council again forbade the use of steam south of 14th Street, and the terminal at Broadway and Wall Street was never built.

Cornelius Vanderbilt began his working career as a boy, operating a ferry between Manhattan and Staten Island, then moved into shipping and railroading.

(The proscription of locomotives subsequently was extended to 26th Street, and then to 42nd Street—the final ban thus determining the location of Grand Central Terminal.)

By 1852, the New York and Harlem had run its first train to Albany. Since the trip took seven hours, as against eighteen for riverboats, the company expected to get rich. But the line's tracks ran far inland from the Hudson through mountainous country. The rival Hudson-River Railroad, chartered in 1846 by a group of Poughkeepsie entrepreneurs, followed the river, made the journey from Chambers and Hudson streets to Albany in five hours, and so got the cream of the business. Meanwhile, wild rate-cutting by the riverboats kept both rail lines from making money.

Then Cornelius Vanderbilt, called "Commodore" because of his success with ships, took over. In the 1850s, he bought heavily into the New York and Harlem, and in the following decade into the Hudson-River line; subsequently he merged the two into the New York Central, which ran from Albany to Buffalo. It was a happy marriage for a century; then competition from trucks, buses, and private automobiles compelled the New York Central to unite with the Pennsylvania Railroad in what became the Penn Central. When the Penn Central went bankrupt, the federally supported Consolidated Railroads Corporation took over the long freight and passenger runs, while the Metropolitan Transportation Authority assumed the task of carrying commuters from the northern suburbs through the tunnels that the New York and Harlem had carved in the granite ridge that bestrode Fourth (Park) Avenue.

The Grand Central Depot, on the site of the present Grand Central Terminal at 42nd Street, opened in 1871.

The Subway That Ran on Wind Power

New York's first subway ran on wind power. Built in secret in 1870 by a virtually forgotten genius, it boasted an elegant, 120-foot-long, underground waiting room adorned with paintings and frescoes, a fountain, settees, a grand piano, and a huge aquarium full of goldfish. The line ran under Broadway from Warren Street to Murray Street—a distance of 312 feet—and its one car, a fancily appointed tubular affair, seated twenty-two people; the car was propelled, ten miles an hour, by a blast of air from a gigantic, stationary, steam-driven fan. When the car reached the end of the line, it tripped a wire that reversed the fan, which sucked the car back to its starting point.

It was not so nutty as it sounds. It was conceived and constructed by Alfred Ely Beach, a brilliant patent attorney, inventor (of the typewriter, among other things), and publisher (his publications included the *Scientific American* and, for a time, a great newspaper, the *Sun*). Beach wanted to relieve the traffic jams of carriages, horsecars, horse-drawn buses, carts and wagons that made his daily trips between his office downtown and his home in Chelsea an hour long. Manhattan's 700,000 people needed mass transportation free of street-surface congestion. Beach ruled out an elevated railway as ugly and decided to go underground. But steam-driven locomotives would fill his tunnels with smoke, so he hit on wind power. (Gasoline engines and electrically powered trains had yet to be invented.) His 312-foot-long subway would demonstrate how the traffic problem could be eased; someday, with more powerful fans, trains would

race beneath the city at perhaps sixty to one hundred miles an hour.

But Beach knew that to build his sample subway, he would have to operate with subterfuge and secrecy, because William Marcy ("Boss") Tweed had a rival plan, for an elevated railway, and he was running the city. So Beach obtained a permit only to construct a small pneumatic tube for shooting mail and packages beneath the streets. Then, in secrecy, he proceeded to dig a subway. He rented the basement of Devlin's Store on Broadway as headquarters, and on June 1, 1869, excavation and construction crews—totaling a dozen men, with Beach himself as superintendent—began work; they tunneled furtively at night beneath Broadway, while wagons with muffled wheels carried off the soil. The project remained undiscovered almost until its completion; then the

New York Herald, its curiosity aroused by the sagging of Broadway's sidewalk, published on January 4, 1870, a story a column and a third in length exposing Beach's venture. Tweed, not surprisingly, was furious, but when Beach officially unveiled his creation the following month, the press and the public waxed ecstatic. "In five minutes, a citizen residing in Harlem can be deposited in the City Hall," one newspaper said, looking ahead optimistically to the line's extension.

In its first year, the block-long subway carried some 400,000 sightseeing passengers, at a quarter a head, and took in $100,000. Beach was ready to build to Central Park, but Tweed saw to it that his puppet governor twice vetoed bills that would have

Working in secrecy, Beach's construction crew extends the tunnel by advancing the shield.

The train approaches the station, where passengers wait to take the brief journey under Broadway.

granted Beach a charter; though Beach kept on fighting, he eventually ran out of money and his subway shut down. Its remains are incorporated in the old City Hall station of the BMT.

Steinway's Non-Musical Tubes

The oldest existing subway tunnels in the city, now used by the IRT's Flushing Line, were dug in 1892 for William Steinway, the piano manufacturer, for whom Steinway Avenue in Queens is named. He began twin tubes intended for trolley cars between Manhattan and Queens, but the Panic of 1893 delayed the project and in 1896 Steinway died. August Belmont, who was responsible for the construction of the first actual subway, begun in 1900, took over the Steinway tubes and completed them in 1907. But they went unused until subway trains began traversing them in 1915.

The "El" That Was Pulled Along by Cables

The city's first elevated railroad, quickly to become known as the El, went into service on Greenwich Street between Cortlandt Street and the Battery in 1868. The cars were hauled by cables powered by stationary steam engines. Steam locomotives replaced the cables in 1871.

The West 11th Street station (right) of the Greenwich Street elevated railroad stood where the tracks turned west. The photograph, snapped in May 1876, after the railroad's extension northward looks north from Perry Street.

The Parlor Car on the IRT

The first and only parlor car on New York's subways was built in 1904 for August Belmont, the financier who organized the Interborough Rapid Transit Construction Company, which built the IRT. The only known private subway car in the world, it was named *Mineola* and contained a bar, a washroom with stained-glass windows, full-length windows for observation, an arched Empire ceiling tinted green, and such amenities as pads against which smokers could strike their matches. Besides its motorman—*Mineola* had its own motor—the car's staff included a white-coated waiter who served caviar and drinks to guests. Belmont fre-

quently played host on the car to "Diamond Jim" Brady and Lillian Russell, Brady's actress paramour; the Astors and the Vanderbilts. After Belmont died, in 1924, the car was stored and forgotten until 1947, when the Board of Transportation, in a burst of efficiency, rediscovered it and sold it for scrap. The scrap dealer preserved the car—minus motor, wheels, and axles, which he sold—and in 1973 the Branford Trolley Museum at East Haven, Connecticut, bought it for $100.

The Start of the IRT

The city's first electrically operated subway line began running in October, 1904, between City Hall and 145th Street, four and a half years after the tunneling started, on March 24, 1900. The line was built for the city by the Interborough Rapid Transit Construction Company and was leased to the Interborough Rapid Transit Company for fifty years beginning April 1, 1903. The first subway to Brooklyn opened for service between Bowling Green and Borough Hall on January 8, 1908. The fare on all subways remained five cents for many years, and keeping it at that rate was for a long time a potent political issue.

The IRT subway under construction in 1904, the year that it began operation.

The Trolleys That Gave the Dodgers Their Name

Electrically operated streetcars, known as trolleys, began running in Manhattan on Third Avenue from 65th Street to Harlem on October 23, 1899, but Brooklyn had had them since 1892: the Dodgers baseball team, then Brooklyn-based, got its name—originally the Trolley Dodgers—from them. (The staid old *Brooklyn Eagle*, for a long time Brooklyn's leading newspaper, scorned the name as undignified, and called the team the Superbas.) At their peak, New York streetcars carried a billion passengers a year over five hundred miles of track, but competition from taxis, which charged the same fare—a nickel—and from motor buses drove the trolley companies into bankruptcy. The last trolley car, owned by the Queensborough Bridge Line, stopped running in 1957.

After car tracks were down (below right), students of Brooklyn's Erasmus Hall High School got lessons in boarding cars (above). Cops rode beside cars' motormen (below) during 1899 strike.

Through the Holland Tunnel on Foot

The only people ever to walk through the Holland Tunnel for pleasure were members of the throngs that attended the dedication ceremonies on November 12, 1927, at the Broome Street entrance plaza in Manhattan and the 12th Street entrance plaza in Jersey City. After the speeches had ended and President Calvin Coolidge had pressed a button in the White House, thousands crowded into the tubes to make the first crossing of the Hudson River on foot; one enthusiast walked the tunnel—a mile and a half from portal to portal and at the time the longest underwater tunnel in the world—seven times before asking a tunnel policeman in Jersey City for directions to the nearest ferry.

Pedestrians finally out of the way, motorists venture into Holland Tunnel on opening day.

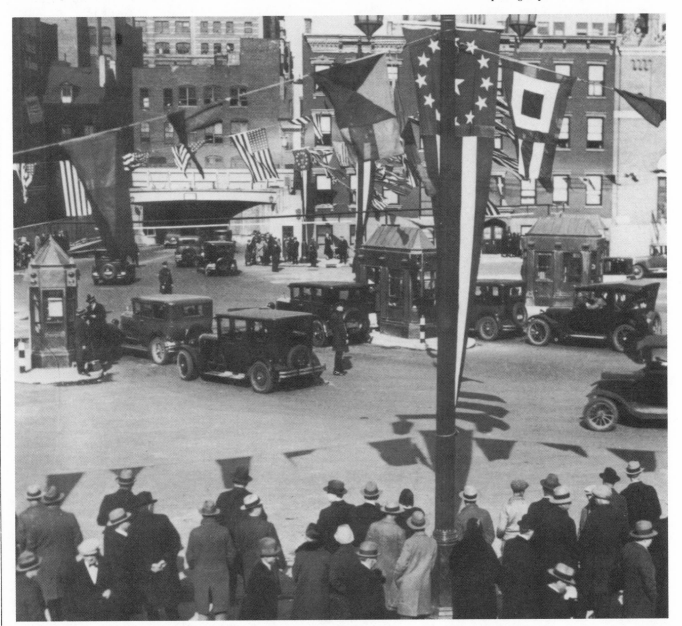

THE THEATER

Shakespeare, As Altered by Cibber

The first known newspaper advertisement of a play in New York appeared in the *Weekly Post-Boy* of February 26, 1750, and announced a performance to be given at a theater at 64-66 Nassau Street. The ad read:

"By his Excellency's Permission, At the Theatre in Nassau Street, On Monday the 5th of March, next, will be presented the Historical Tragedy

of

King Richard 3rd!

"Wrote originally by Shakespeare, and altered by Colley Cibber, Esquire. In this play are contained the Death of King Henry 6th; the artful acquisition of the crown by King Richard, the murder of the Princes in the Tower; the landing of the Earl of Richmond, and the Battle of Bosworth Field.

"Tickets will be ready to be delivered by Thursday next, and to be had of the printer hereof.

"Pitt, five shillings; Gallery, three shillings. To begin precisely at half an hour after six o'clock, and no person to be admitted behind the scenes."

Neither the producer, the director nor the cast was mentioned.

The Careful Critic

The first (and rather timorous) theater review published in New York appeared in the *Weekly Post-Boy* of September 24, 1750. It read:

"On Thursday evening the tragedy of 'Cato' was played at the theatre in this city, before a very numerous audience, the greater part of whom were of the opinion that it was pretty well performed. As it was the fullest assembly that has ever appeared in that house, it may serve to prove that the taste of this place is not so vitiated or lost to a sense of liberty, but that they can prefer a representation of Virtue to one of loose character. 'The Recruiting Officer' will be presented this evening."

The review carried no byline.

The Song on the Bowery

The famous Jewish song, *Eili, Eili,* was first sung at the Windsor Theatre on the Bowery in 1896. The composer was Jacob Sandler.

Sheet music for Eili Eili.

The Beginning of the Black Theater

The first New York theater for blacks only was established in 1821: it was the African Grove Theater at Bleecker and Mercer streets. Its audiences consisted of free blacks, who attended such plays as *Richard III* and *Othello* there and spent intermissions sipping drinks in the theater's garden.

The first great American black actor, Ira Aldridge (c. 1807-1867) made his stage debut in adolescence at the African Grove Theater, near where he grew up. But he achieved fame, wealth and numerous royal decorations for his Shakespearean roles in England, Ireland, Saxony, Prussia, Austria, Switzerland, Russia and Poland. (He is shown above as Othello.) Aldridge eventually took British citizenship, and a chair was named in his honor at the Shakespeare Memorial Theater in Stratford-upon-Avon. Aldridge died in Poland.

Lorenzo da Ponte

Opening Night at the Opera

The first grand opera ever presented in full in its original language in New York—and America—was Rossini's *The Barber of* *Seville.* It was sung before an audience of unprecedented elegance at the Park Theatre on Park Row on November 29, 1825; the stars were the Garcia family—husband, wife, son, and daughter—who had been enticed here from London for $30,000 raised by a wine merchant and opera buff named Dominick Lynch. Twenty-two local musicians made up the orchestra. Flitting between the audience out front and the singers backstage was Lorenzo da Ponte, the librettist for some of Mozart's operas, and a friend of Lynch's. (Da Ponte was an Italian Jew who had converted to Catholicism and studied for the priesthood. He came to New York from London in 1806 to escape his creditors, and opened a vegetable shop on

Dominick Lynch

the Bowery. Later he taught Italian at Columbia University.) After the performance, the *New York Evening Post* predicted that the city would never again be without grand opera.

Ornate interior of the Park Theatre, with its large stage, was the locale of the city's first full opera performance.

ARCHITECTURE

The Conference House

The first peace conference of the Revolutionary War was held on Staten Island in September 1776—when the war was just getting started—in the building (right) now known as the Conference House. Benjamin Franklin, John Adams and Edward Rutledge represented the Americans, and Admiral Richard Howe and his brother, General William Howe, the British. Though the admiral was sympathetic to the Americans, the negotiations, of course, got nowhere. The Conference House was built in 1680 by the British naval captain Christopher Billopp, whose circumnavigation of Staten Island established the island as part of New York rather than New Jersey. Billopp was rewarded with a grant of 1,163 Staten Island acres, amid which he erected his house.

The Way-Out Apartment House

The city's first luxury apartment house, The Dakota, rose in 1884 at 72nd Street and Central Park West and, despite the construction of hundreds of splendid condominiums and co-ops in recent years, still epitomizes elegance in New York life. Financed by Edward Clark of the Singer Sewing Machine fortune, and designed by Henry J. Hardenbergh, The Dakota contains 65 apartments that vary in size from four to twenty rooms. It is now owned by its occupants. The Dakota derives its name from the circumstance that when it was built, no one who mattered lived north of 59th Street and skeptics suggested that the building might as well have been sited in the Dakota territory.

The Dakota looks down on Central Park ice-skaters.

The Great Glass Slide

The city's first office building (right) with a facade that billows outward toward its base stands at 9 West 57th Street, where it towers over its more conventional neighbors, and resembles an outsize ocean wave. The structure, designed by Skidmore, Owings and Merrill, went up in 1972; it now has several look-alikes.

Painted bright red, and nine feet high, the address of 9 West 57th Street is not easily missed.

The Stolen Landmark

The Bogardus Building (above), was the first in the city with a full cast-iron facade. It was one of five constructed in 1849 by James Bogardus at 258-262 Washington Street. (James Bogardus was a descendant of the Rev. Everardus Bogardus, New Amsterdam's second dominie.) It was the first structure as well in which the walls bore no weight—permitting large windows—and thus was a forerunner of the skyscraper. But, alas, it was also the first building in the city to be stolen. Twice. After it was razed in 1971, thieves made off with two-thirds of its cast-iron panels, which the Landmarks Preservation Commission had stored in a lot for possible use in reconstruction of the building on a new site. The Commission put the rest under lock and key in a warehouse, whence those relics too disappeared.

Zeus never slept here.

Temple in the Sky

The first—and only—simulated Greek temple to adorn the city's skyline sat anachronistically and incongruously atop 50-52 Wall Street. A penthouse of forgotten gods, the structure could best be seen from the air. The building was erected in 1928 for the National City Company, forerunner of Citicorp, by the architectural firm of McKim, Mead & White. To the dismay of many admirers, it was demolished in 1981, to be replaced by a building called 60 Wall Street, owned by the Bank of New York. The temple's presence reflected the architectural predilections of the 1910s and 1920s, when the classical style was the order of the decade.

The City's Other Skyline

For the first half of the 20th century, "New York's skyline" meant the awesome sight of lower Manhattan's spires and towers. The author of this book once met in England a young woman who said she would be happy to sail to New York and back without getting off the ship, just to relish the view from the harbor.

There is another skyline now for her to see, though it would not be visible from the bay. It was born in midtown in 1930, with the rise of the Chrysler Building (opposite, right, with spire), which was the first anywhere to surpass the Eiffel Tower in height. But its reign as the world's tallest structure proved brief. The Empire State Building (opposite, left), going up almost simultaneously topped the Chrysler by the addition of the world's first dirigible mooring mast on a skyscraper. (The mast has never been used.)

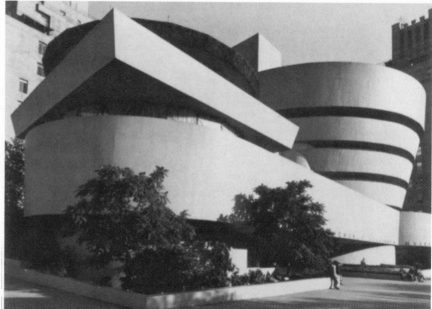

Wright or Wrong

The first—and only—New York building designed by Frank Lloyd Wright is the Guggenheim Museum (above) on Fifth Avenue at 89th Street. It is also one of the city's more controversial edifices; detractors have likened its external form to that of a parking garage and have suggested that visitors be equipped with roller skates to whisk down its internal ramps, but the *AIA Guide to New York*, sponsored by the American Institute of Architects, describes the building's central space as ". . . one of the greatest modern interiors of the world: a museum more important as architecture than for the contents it displays." In any case, art-lovers have to stand on sloping floors to look at rectilinear paintings hung on rounded walls. One acerbic explanation for the structure's design is that Wright, a midwesterner, intended it as a joke on a city that was less than enthusiastic about his unorthodox architecture.

The nascent skyline developed first signs of its now dramatic diversity with the construction of the United Nations Secretariat Building (below foreground) on the East River shore, a site once dominated by slaughterhouses. New York's first building with walls entirely of glass, it was designed in 1952 by a group of the world's pre-eminent architects, including Le Corbusier of France, Oscar Niemeyer of Brazil and America's Wallace K. Harrison. To the right of the U.N. Building and almost on a line with the Chrysler Building stands One United Nations Plaza, a shimmering hotel-cum-office building finished in 1976.

The Pan Am Building at the extreme right, the flat top of which was a heliport until a disastrous accident in 1977, was also designed by a group, this one headed by Walter Gropius. For many years before he came to America in 1937, Gropius was the guiding spirit of Germany's Bauhaus, the birthplace of the International Style of architecture. That style informs most of New York's recent construction, some of it born of hasty liaison with the city's idiosyncratic building code.

Whatever the merits and demerits that the beholder's eye detects in individual structures, though, the total of the mid-city skyline exceeds the sum of its parts: it would, no doubt, impress that young woman from England.

VITAL STATISTICS

The First-Born

The first white child born in New Netherland was Jean Vigné, whose parents, Guillaume and Adrienne Cuville Vigné, came from Valenciennes, which is now part of France. Jean's actual birth date is unknown; European travelers who met him in 1679 said that he was "about sixty-five," which would make 1614 the year of his birth. But New Netherland had not yet been settled then, though fur traders commuted from Europe. More likely, Jean was the first of the 1624 bumper baby crop at Fort Amsterdam. In any case, his name pops up occasionally in early records. On June 21, 1651, he was appointed manager of the sizable Damen Plantation, and a few years later he filed an official complaint that the construction of a city wall had damaged the property. Governor Stuyvesant granted him a new fence. Except for one incident in 1656, when he was accused of smuggling beer, he seems to have led a more or less exemplary life: he served for a time as *schepen* (which can be translated as alderman, magistrate, or sheriff), as alternate commissioner of the road to Harlem, and as inspector of the Common Strand fence on the East River shore. Apparently he was a bachelor, and lived with a sister until his death in 1689.

Sarah of Wallabout

The first white girl born in what is now New York was for a long time thought to have been Sarah Rapalje, whose father, Joris Jansen Rapalje, a Walloon, settled on 335 acres in Brooklyn's Wallabout area (Dutch *wall*, meaning Walloon, and *bocht*, meaning bay) when Peter Minuit was the colony's director general. (A family tradition has it that Minuit and a friend, hunting, stopped in at the Rapalje house for lunch, found no one home, and devoured the only edibles in sight—Indian dumplings. When Mrs. Rapalje—an ex-Parisienne whose maiden name was Catalyna Trico—returned from the fields with Sarah, she berated Minuit so vehemently that he promised her a cow to shut her up. He kept his word.) But Sarah, alas, was no native of the city: she was born June 9, 1625, at Fort Orange (now Albany) and did not come downriver until she was three. However, she produced a lot of natives: she bore seven children to Hans Hansen Bergen and, after he died, seven more to Theunis Gysbert Bogaert. Bergens and Bogaerts, as well as Rapaljes, Rapalies, and Rapalyeas, long abounded here. (Catalyna Rapalje bore 11 children, of whom Sarah was the first, and had 149 grandchildren.) The identity of the first white girl born in the area, though, remains undetermined.

The De Conincs' Civil Wedding

The first recorded marriage in Fort Amsterdam took place on

The Secret Presidential Wedding

The first—and only—secret wedding of a President of the United States took place in New York's Church of the Ascension at 10th Street and Fifth Avenue on June 26, 1844. (The church is still there, though the meadow that surrounded it is not.) The ceremony united President John Tyler, fifty-four, and Julia Gardiner, twenty-four, the daughter of David Gardiner, of Gardiners Island, off the eastern end of Long Island. When news of the marriage leaked, it caused a good deal of shocked chatter: The President, a widower and the father of seven children, was deemed much too old to take such a young bride. The *New York Evening Post*, though, recorded the marriage with astonishing self-restraint; on

John Tyler

September 23, 1639, between Thomas de Coninc and Marritje Frans van Beets. The ceremony was performed by the governor, Willem Kieft, and the council rather than by the dominie, the Reverend Everardus Bogardus. Kieft and Bogardus greatly disliked each other; ironically, they died in the same shipwreck on the way to Holland

The De Conincs, however, presumably lived happily ever after, for history does not mention them again.

The Adoption of Anthony Angola

The first legal adoption of a child by a black couple occurred in 1661. Emanuel Pietersen and his wife Dorothy Angola, both of whom were free citizens, petitioned in court "that a certificate of Freedom may be granted for a lad named Anthony Angola, whom they adopted when an infant and have since reared and educated". The Pietersens paid 300 guilders for the youngster.

The Marriage on the Water

Though hundreds of thousands of ships have sailed in and out of New York Harbor since Giovanni da Verrazano's *Delfina* in May, 1524, and though shipboard marriages are no great rarities, the first wedding known to have taken place on the waters of the bay dates only to September 21, 1975. The ceremony, performed in wind and rain on the upper deck of the 19th Century Norwegian *Barba Negra,* lying off the Statue of Liberty, united Baron Erwin Schacky of the German foreign service and Mary Ellen McGough. The *Barba Negra's* skipper, Captain Gary Schwisow, officiated. The ship's crew wore gold earrings and whale's tooth necklaces, the guests jeans and slickers, and the bride her grandmother's wedding veil. The wedding party had boarded the *Barba Negra* at the South Street Seaport.

The First Black Church Wedding

The first blacks to be married in a church were Anthony van Angola, a widower, and Lucie d'Angola, a widow. The ceremony took place on May 5, 1641, in the original St. Nicholas, the church in the fort. From then on, church weddings were *de rigueur* for black people.

an inside page, in type the size generally used nowadays for classified ads, it wrote:

MARRIED: In this city, on Wednesday the 26th inst., at the Church of the Ascension, by the Right Reverend Benjamin T. Onderdonck, Bishop of the Eastern Diocese of New York, his Excellency JOHN TYLER, President of the United States, to JULIA GARDINER, eldest daughter of the late DAVID GARDINER, ESQ.

In a follow-up story the next day, the *Evening Post*—again on an inside page and at the bottom of a column—announced:

The President's Marriage: We are requested to state that, in order to insure the privacy so much desired by the bride and her family in their affliction, it was deemed proper that not even the nearest relatives and connexions of the parties, beyond their immediate families, should be advised of the event. Contrary to reports in the newspapers generally, the bridal party consisted only of the President and his bride, her mother, sister, and two brothers and Mr. J. Tyler, Jr.

The "affliction" mentioned by the *Evening Post* had brought the couple together: it was the death of the bride's father. A cannon had exploded on the new warship *Princeton* while the President and Gardiner, who was a friend of his, were inspecting the vessel; Gardiner was killed and Tyler himself narrowly escaped. The scandalmongers need not have concerned themselves with the couple's disparate ages; Tyler fathered seven more children by Julia before he died in 1862 at age seventy-two.

Julia Gardiner Tyler

CRIMES AND VIOLENCE

The Murder in the Harbor

The first homicide recorded in the metropolitan area occurred on September 6, 1609, two days after crewmen from Henry Hudson's *Half Moon* first set foot ashore on Coney Island (as tradition has it) or on Sandy Hook (as a diary of the voyage implies). The victim was John Colman, an Englishman and a longtime shipmate of Hudson. Colman and four seamen from the *Half Moon* were taking soundings from a small boat late that afternoon when two Indian canoes approached, one carrying fourteen braves, the other twelve. Though the Indians hitherto had been "very civill" and had seemed "very glad of our coming," as a ship's officer noted, a fight broke out when rain and darkness fell. Colman got a fatal arrow through the throat, and two of his shipmates were wounded. The survivors rowed all night before they found the *Half Moon*. Colman was buried September 7 on Sandy Hook, and Hudson named the grave site Colman's Point.

Escorted by Indian canoes, Henry Hudson's Half Moon sails up the river after the death of John Colman.

The Happy-Ending Hanging

The first public hanging took place in Hanover Square in 1641, but the incident had a happy ending. Some Dutch West India Company slaves had killed another slave, Jan Premero, and the authorities arrested nine suspects and threatened them with torture if they did not name the killers. All nine then proclaimed themselves guilty, figuring that the company would not damage nine valuable pieces of property and would let them off lightly. But Governor Willem Kieft, equally wily, ordered them to draw lots to determine which one should be hanged. A gigantic black named Manuel Gerrit lost, and the whole town, plus some sightseeing Indians, turned out for his execution. The gallows was a ladder propped against a wall of Fort Amsterdam. Gerrit, chanting the while, was made to climb to the top rung and two ropes were put around his neck. Then the ladder was pulled away. But the ropes broke and Gerrit plunged to the ground. As Gerrit writhed in pain, Kieft instructed the hangman, a black named Pieter, to find heavier ropes. But the spectacle had proved too strong for Fort Amsterdam stomachs; sobbing women and ordinarily stoic men beseeched Kieft to let Gerrit go. So Gerrit was turned loose with an admonition to stay out of trouble. Apparently he did, for three years later a Manuel Gerrit was one of eleven blacks emancipated in recognition of their service to the company. Gerrit became one of Greenwich Village's earliest landholders.

Dominie Bogardus embarks for Holland August 17, 1647, to testify against Kieft, who boarded same ship.

The Near-Assassination of Willem Kieft

The first attempt to kill a public official took place in 1642, and the target deservedly was Willem Kieft, the director general, or governor. An Indian-hater, Kieft had instigated a number of massacres—an angry dove among the Fort Amsterdam hawks charged that "[Indian] infants were torn from their mothers' breasts and hacked to pieces in the presence of their parents." An Indian chief confided to a white friend, Captain David de Vries, that his young braves were restive for revenge because "one had lost his father, another his mother, a third his uncle and also their friends" in attacks by whites. De Vries suggested that the chief talk to Kieft. The chief did—and Kieft told him that if he would have

the malcontents killed, Kieft would pay him "two hundred fathoms of seawant"—strings of high-grade wampum totaling 1,200 feet in length and worth nearly 800 guilders (currently $400—a high price indeed for those pre-Mafia days). De Vries, who was present, "laughed within myself that the Indian should kill his friends . . . to gratify us." The chief politely rejected the proposal but promised to try to keep the peace. Not long afterward, his angry young men wiped out scores of suburbanites, including Anne Hutchinson, for whom the Hutchinson River and the parkway are named.

Terrified by the Indian attacks, the surviving colonists demanded Kieft's removal and arrest. Kieft

tried to shift the blame to a henchman, Maryn Adriaensen, a prosperous thug who had led much of the slaughter of Indians while Kieft warmed himself by his own fireside. Enraged at Kieft's perfidy, Adriaensen went to his home and attacked him with a pistol and a cutlass. Adriaensen was disarmed and locked up. Two of Adriaensen's supporters then went to Kieft to demand Adriaensen's release. When Kieft rebuffed them, one of the pair, Jacob Slough, fired a pistol twice at Kieft. He missed both times and a sentry shot him dead. Slough's head was displayed on the town gallows. Adriaensen was shipped back to Amsterdam for trial, but the disposition of the case went unrecorded. Kieft himself drowned in a shipwreck on the way to the Netherlands to defend himself against charges resulting from his bloodthirstiness. Another victim of the shipwreck was the Reverend Everardus Bogar-who was the most important witness against Kieft. Kieft's death opened the way for the appointment of Peter Stuyvesant as governor.

The Sheriff Who Took the Ferry

The first law-enforcement officer to become a convicted criminal was Jan Teunissen, sheriff of Brooklyn. On October 12, 1648—not yet designated Columbus Day—he was found guilty of stealing a ferryboat from the Dutch West India Company, and of slander. The details are not recorded. Teunissen was sentenced to work 100 days for the company and 50 days for the church without pay, and to put up bail during the 150 days.

DISASTERS

The 674-Building Fire

The city's greatest fire started in zero-degree weather at 9 a.m. on December 16, 1835, in the Comstock & Adams drygoods store near Hanover and Pearl streets. It destroyed virtually everything south of Wall Street and east of Broadway: 674 buildings burned, at a loss of twenty million dollars, among them the elegant Merchants Exchange, the Custom House, and the Dutch church that bore a plaque with Governor Willem Kieft's name on it. In the nineteen-hour-long battle against the blaze, many firemen—scores of whom had ferried their engines from Brooklyn and Jersey City—suffered injuries that maimed them for life.

As lower Manhattan burned, an artist perched atop the Bank of America building at Wall and William streets recorded the catastrophe.

The Tragedy of the General Slocum

The city's most spectacular disaster and the one that took the most lives occurred in the East River on June 15, 1904; the gleaming, three-deck side-wheeler *General Slocum*, "Queen of the Excursion Steamers," caught fire soon after it departed from its East Third Street pier carrying 1,335 passengers bound for a picnic at Locust Grove on Huntington Bay. Most were children from the Sunday school of St. Mark's Lutheran Church on the Lower East Side. There would have been four more passengers, but Mrs. Philip Straub of St. Mark's Place debarked with her three youngsters just before the vessel steamed away. "We are doomed, I know it, I feel it," she told her friends. "Don't go. I beg you, don't go." The *General Slocum* was off 125th Street when a small boy, pointing toward the bow, told a ticket-taker, "Mister, I saw smoke there." The ticket-taker replied, "Beat it, kid." Minutes later, off 130th Street, flames—which originated in a paint storage locker—enveloped the lower deck. August Schneider's band kept playing while fire hoses burst in the crew's hands, sand buckets turned out to be empty, and women threw their children overboard in life jackets that disintegrated when they hit the water. Schneider finally dived into the river himself, turned toward the ship, caught an infant tossed from an upper deck, and swam to a tugboat. Captain Willam van Schaick, sixty-eight, who had received an award the year before for carrying 35 million passengers safely, kept the *General Slocum* going at full steam ahead: he dared not head for the Bronx shore for fear of setting oil tanks and lumber yards ablaze and he could not turn to starboard because of submerged rocks in the river. The whole vessel was burning and the upper deck had collapsed before Van Schaick finally ran the ship aground on a sand bar twenty yards off North Brother Island. (Two petty thieves, breaking rock on nearby Rikers Island, raced for a rowboat with a guard in pursuit, and rescued fifteen people before the guards took them back to the rock pile.) Of the 1,335 passengers—who represented 622 families—1,051 perished and 124 were injured; only 160 escaped unscathed. Van Schaick, although he maintained that he had behaved correctly under the circumstances, was sent to jail for three years. After the disaster the whole steamboat inspection system was revised.

The wreck of the General Slocum *rests on a sandbar in the river. North Brother Island is in background.*

COMMUNICATIONS

Unlisted Number

The first private telephone in the city was installed in May of 1877 at 89 Fifth Avenue by order of a Mr. Charles Cheever, acting on behalf of a friend whose name he did not give.

The Commercial That Started It All

The first radio commercial was broadcast by A.T.&T.'s station WEAF (now NBC's station WNBC) on August 28, 1922. It plugged the Queensboro Corporation's Hawthorne Court garden apartments in Jackson Heights, Queens. Maxwell Blackwell, Queensboro's sales manager, wrote the script, which he took ten minutes to deliver, and which Queensboro's staff described as "a ten-minute filibuster." The time cost $100, and the commercial went on the air once a week for several weeks, getting a "fair response." The Hawthorne Court apartments are still chipper.

Control room of WEAF in 1940.

The Two-Page Phone Book

The first telephone directory was issued October 25, 1878; it consisted of two pages headed "List of Subscribers to the Central Office System of the Bell Telephone Company of New York." By 1880, the directory included 2,800 names.

Alexander Graham Bell's first telephone transmitter (above) over which he summoned his assistant in 1876, and (right) the first New York telephone directory.

B-U-L-O-V-A Watch Time

The first authorized spot televison commercial went on the air on July 1, 1941, from an early TV station designated WNBT. It consisted of an announcement: "It is now one twenty-nine and fifty seconds, B-U-L-O-V-A, Bulova watch time," which was followed by a short plug for Bulova watches. The pioneer TV advertiser was John H. Ballard, who was president of Bulova.

AMENITIES

The Paving of Stone Street

The first street pavement was laid in 1658 on what became Stone Street between Whitehall and Broad streets. The street was originally named Brouwer (Brewer) Street, because Oloff Stevenson Van Cortlandt operated a brewery there. But the brewery horses raised so much dust, dirtying windows and curtains, that Mrs. Van Cortlandt and her neighbors demanded that the city pave the street. The job was completed three years later, with cobblestones as the pavement. The residents paid the cost.

Stone Street gets a cobblestone pavement, the first of any kind in the city.

The Sidewalks for Broadway

The city's first sidewalks were laid in 1790 on Broadway between Vesey and Murray streets. Of brick and stone, they were barely wide enough to permit two people to walk abreast.

My Son, The Doctor

The city's first hospital was established in 1660, at the urging of Jacob Hendricksen Varrevange, a surgeon, to tend "sick soldiers and Negroes." It occupied two buildings erected for it, and one of its physicians, Dr. Lucas Santomee, was the city's first black doctor; he was the son of a slave, Peter Santomee, who had arrived here in 1625 or 1626 and was emancipated two decades later.

Not-So-Clean Sweeps

The first street-cleaning contract was awarded by the city in 1696, at £30 a year; it was intended to relieve householders of the responsibility for keeping streets clean in front of their houses. The new system did not work, so another was tried in 1702. Residents had to sweep up street dirt in heaps in front of their doors every Friday morning for removal by cartmen by Saturday night; the cartmen got either three or six cents a load, depending on whether the householder or the cartman shoveled it onto the cart.

The first modern street-cleaning and garbage-collection system was instituted in 1895, when Colonel George E. Waring, street-cleaning commissioner under a reform mayor, organized a force of "White Wings"—so called because of their neat white uniforms. A song, "White Wings," and a Broadway play, of the same name, were written about them.

White Wing wields his broom, June 12, 1896, at 48th Street and Seventh Avenue.

The Lights of Manhattan

Street lighting was introduced in New York in 1697, when an ordinance required that "every seventh householder, in the dark time of the moon, cause a lantern and candle to be hung out of his window on a pole, the expense to be divided among the seven families." Aldermen were charged with enforcing the ordinance.

The first gas pipeline, through which flowed gas made from coal, was laid in May of 1825, and extended up Broadway from the Bowery to Canal Street. It was built by the New York Gas-light Company, incorporated in 1823. Gas proved so popular that in 1830 the Manhattan Gas-light Company was incorporated to supply the rest of Manhattan. The first private house to use gas was the residence of Samuel Treadwell at 29 East Fourth Street, built in 1830 in what was then one of the best neighborhoods in town. (The house survives as a landmark known as the Old Merchant's House, and the two gas companies merged into what became Consolidated Edison.)

The first street lighting by electricity was provided in 1880, along Broadway from 14th Street to 26th Street, by the Brush Electric Illuminating Company, which used arc lamps invented by Charles Francis Brush. Simultaneously, Thomas Alva Edison was perfecting the incandescent light bulb and selling stock in the Edison Electric Illuminating Company, which intended to supply light to houses and shops. Edison's first central generating plant began humming, on one dynamo, at 3 p.m. on September 4, 1882, at 257 Pearl Street. Edison himself turned on the lights that afternoon in the office of his richest customer, J. Pierpont Morgan, at Broad and Wall streets. Morgan, along with Edison's other patrons, got his electricity free for several months.

Dynamo room of Edison's generating plant, shown below shortly after it began operation, provided electric lighting for houses and shops, as distinct from street lamps. Before conservation of energy became essential, all Manhattan (right) glowed at night.

Sangria in the Garden

The first sangria was served about 1760 at the Vauxhall Gardens, at Greenwich and Warren streets, an establishment owned for a time by Samuel Fraunces of Fraunces Tavern. The drink was called "sangaree" and consisted of sweetened red wine flavored with nutmeg and diluted with water. Fraunces may have brought the recipe from his native West Indies. A visiting Philadelphian, Hannah Callender, wrote home that she had drunk "sangaree" while sitting in a bower at the gardens, from which she had "a fine view of the North River down as far as Sandy Hook."

The Long-Lived Library

The city's first library was established in 1700 in the second City Hall (where Federal Hall now stands) at the instance of Lord Bellomont, the British governor. A descendant survives: Bellomont's library was incorporated into another, organized in 1754 by prominent New Yorkers, and the resulting institution was named the City Library, which King George III chartered in 1772 as the New York Society Library. British troops looted the collection during the Revolution, but after the war the library's surviving books were gathered and returned to the City Hall. The library moved in 1795 to Nassau Street, and, after a number of other moves, the New York Society Library thrives in a landmark house at 53 East 79th Street. Governor Bellomont's original collection has grown to 200,000 volumes.

Legends of the Martini

The first cocktail, a Martini, was mixed in the days of New Amsterdam in Pieter Laurenzen Kock's tavern at No. 1 Broadway, according to an undocumented tale. But Betsy Flanagan, who ran a tavern on the road between Tarrytown and White Plains in Revolutionary times, always claimed that the cocktail originated at her place: General George Washington's Yankees provided the gin, she said, and General Jean Baptiste Donatien de Vimeur Rochambeau's Frenchmen brought the vermouth, when Rochambeau joined Washington near Tarrytown in July, 1781. The mixture was stirred with a feather from the tail of Betsy Flanagan's pet red rooster, and the cocktail was born.

The Pioneer Chestnut Man

The first vendor of roasted chestnuts, a Frenchman, set himself up at Broadway and Duane Street in 1828. Though few knew his name, he stood at his post for so many years that he became something of a landmark.

The Gayetty Contribution to Civilization

The world's first toilet paper was produced in New York in 1857 by Joseph C. Gayetty of 154 West 33rd Street. It was pearl-colored manila paper made of hemp. Gayetty, who watermarked his name into each sheet, advertised it as "Gayetty's Medicated Paper—a perfectly pure article for the toilet and for the prevention of piles." Five hundred sheets cost fifty cents.

The Ambulance from Bellevue

The city's first hospital-run ambulance service was established at Bellevue Hospital in 1869. The hospital gets its name from Belle Vue Farm, the estate of Lindley Murray, on which the hospital rose between 1811 and 1816; since 1794, yellow-fever patients had been isolated at the farm. Bellevue antedates its name, however; it originated as a six-bed infirmary on the site of the present City Hall. The infirmary shared a building with a poorhouse and a jail.

First passenger elevator encountered considerable skepticism: the caption on this contemporary lithograph was "A Death Trap."

The Lift on Lower Broadway

The world's first workable, dependable passenger elevator was installed in the five-story Haughwout Building at 488-492 Broadway by Elisha Graves Otis on March 23, 1857, three years after Otis had established the Otis Elevator Company in Yonkers. Steam-powered, the elevator rose forty feet a minute and cost $300 to build. It lasted half a century and a souvenir of it survives: a door in the Broadway facade of the building, which is still there, is surmounted by a sign ELEVATOR, and just behind the door is a working elevator shaft.

The Electric Advertisement

The first big electrically lit advertisement of the kind that made Broadway the Great White Way was turned on in June of 1892 on a nine-story skyscraper at Broadway and 23rd Street; its 1,457 white, blue, red, and green bulbs, set in a frame 60 by 68 feet, flashed the advice

BUY HOMES ON
LONG ISLAND
SWEPT BY OCEAN BREEZES
MANHATTAN BEACH
ORIENTAL HOTEL
MANHATTAN HOTEL
GILMORE'S BAND
BROOK'S FIREWORKS

The lights went out at 11 p.m.

He Put Her Name in Lights

The first neon advertising sign, installed on the marquee of the Cosmopolitan Theatre at Columbus Circle in July of 1923, plugged Marion Davies, who was starring in the show "Little Old New York." Note to people under forty: Marion Davies was an actress of debatable talent, but as the long-time mistress of publisher William Randolph Hearst, she always got a lot of publicity—in Hearst's newspapers—for her stage appearances.

Marion Davies

How Pastrami Came to New York

The first pastrami-on-rye-to-go slid over the counter in a Delancey Street delicatessen in 1888. Its advent is described authoritatively by Patricia Volk Blitzer:

"My great-grandfather, Sussman Volk, arrived in this country about 100 years ago from Lithuania, where he was a miller. But he found the wheat business in America too much of a grind so after a while he became a tinker, traveling from town to town to peddle the pots and pans he carried on his back. One night he wound up in New Rochelle with lots of pots and pans but no place to stay until, finally, a kind householder let him sleep on straw in the stable. Next morning, as he was *dovening*—that is, praying—in the stable, it occurred to Sussman that his current way of life lacked dignity. As a religious Jew, he of course knew how to butcher meat, so he opened a small butcher shop on the Lower East Side. Naturally, the shop had a large icebox and Sussman—or Reb Sussel, as he was known—used to let a Rumanian friend store meat in it without charge. But the Rumanian was not too happy with America and decided to return home; he was probably the only one who ever did. Before leaving, he repaid Great-Grandfather for his favor by giving him the recipe for pastrami. Pastrami proved such a hit with Reb Sussel's customers that in 1888 he opened New York's first delicatessen at 88 DeLancey Street—it's a bank now, I think—and sold the first over-the-counter pastrami sandwich. He prospered and his delicatessen became, it's safe to say, the Maxim's of the Lower East Side."

The last of the Volks,*, Mrs. Blitzer—a writer—adds that "at the risk of forsaking my heritage and incurring an evil eye, I must confess that my favorite deli sandwich is ham on rye with mayo." *Sussman Volk's son Jacob, Mrs. Blitzer's grandfather, deserted the delicatessen counter to become what James Thurber described in The Years With Ross as "a building wrecker out of Herculean mythology, who tore down two hundred and fifty big structures in Manhattan during his lifetime and never passed the Woolworth Building but what he dreamed of the joys of razing it." The New Yorker was preparing a profile of Jacob Volk shortly before he died; the profile was abandoned but Thurber noted Volk's death in a lengthy item in the Talk of the Town.

Bagels, sans lox and cheese.

The Bagel from Clinton Street

The first bagel baked in New York emerged from a cellar at 15 Clinton Street in 1896, according to Label Vishinsky, inventor of an automatic bagelmaker and a leading authority on bagels. The bagel was introduced to New York from Philadelphia, but, says Vishinsky, it was already an ancient institution. It originated in fourteenth-century Germany as an adjunct of the hunt; after huntsmen had slain a boar or a stag, they boiled a lump of dough, fashioned it in the shape of a *Steigbügel* (stirrup), and used it to adorn their prize at the table. The word "bagel," however, derives from Yiddish: *beig* means "bend," and its diminutive, *beigl*, means "small arc." History has failed to record the date of the bagel's first union with lox and cream cheese.

Pastrami on rye.

Dr. Hosack's Elgin Garden

The city's first botanical garden opened in 1801 on the site of the Radio City Music Hall, the RCA Building, and the Channel Gardens in Rockefeller Center, and soon won international esteem. It was the passionate hobby and philanthropy of Dr. David Hosack, the New York-born physician who attended the dying Alexander Hamilton after Hamilton's duel with Aaron Burr. A teacher at the College of Physicians and Surgeons and a professor of botany at Columbia College at a time when medical science leaned heavily on the therapeutic properties of plants, Dr. Hosack established the garden as a place of study for future doctors as well as a delight for the public; he named it for his father's birthplace, Elgin, in Scotland. Dr. Hosack paid the city $4,807 for the twenty acres that the garden encompassed and spent some $110,000 more on erecting a greenhouse and a couple of hothouses and on stocking them and the surrounding land with trees, shrubs, herbs and other plants from all over the world. The collection included gifts from the Jardin des Plantes in Paris—arranged by Thomas Jefferson—and from London's Linnaean Society, which was headed by a friend of Dr. Hosack. But the garden was pretty far out of town; no one wanted to help pay for its upkeep, and Dr. Hosack could not bear the financial burden indefinitely. After a good deal of lobbying in Albany, Dr. Hosack persuaded the legislature in 1810 to take over the garden for its assessed valuation, $75,000—which he had to wait a long time to receive. And the state declined to spend anything on maintaining the garden; instead, it bestowed the treasure on Columbia College in 1814, in compensation for vast acreage that the college had had to cede to New Hampshire in settlement of a New York-New Hampshire boundary dispute. The struggling college would rather have had money, and it accepted the garden reluctantly. By 1824, only traces remained of the Elgin Garden's once great beauty. But Columbia still owns the land, which it leases to Rockefeller Center; the rent under the current contract, signed in 1974 and running to 1994, started at $9 million a year and rises $200,000 annually to $13 million.

The Channel Gardens (above) in Rockefeller Center occupy part of the site of Dr. Hosack's Elgin Garden (below).

The Forest Primeval in the Bronx

The last relics of the splendid forest that blanketed Manhattan when the white man first arrived survive precariously on forty acres along the Bronx River gorge in the New York Botanical Garden in The Bronx. The trees, stately Canadian hemlocks, rise on one of the few sites in the nation that have never been logged; in the early days of settlement, they escaped destruction only because they were too difficult to get at, but beginning in 1792 they were protected by the Lorillard family, which acquired the grove and more than 600 surrounding acres, on part of which they operated a snuff factory. The city bought the Lorillard property in 1884 and subsequently turned over 400 acres to the New York Botanical Garden. The virgin forest, which dates back to the end of the Ice Age some 20,000 years ago, has suffered from drought, air pollution, vandalism, fires, disease, and—most of all—the well-intentioned interest of human admirers. The tramping feet of visitors damaged the trees' roots, and, to reduce the danger of fire, the botanical garden swept the forest soil of the carpet of natural litter which nurtured new growth. But the garden has launched a program to reverse the process of decline and restore the Forest Primeval in the Bronx.

Once thick with Canadian hemlock, the primeval forest (right) has been invaded by other species. But the hemlocks still retain some of their land.

INDEX

Picture Credits

Abbreviations: LC, Library of Congress, Prints and Photographs Division; MCNY, Museum of the City of New York; NYHS, New-York Historical Society; NYPL, New York Public Library. Title page: Philadelphia Museum of Art, given by the New York Life Insurance Co., photograph by Will Brown; 5: American Banknote Company, Courtesy of Primary Design Galleries, Ltd. 6: William Rivelli. 8: top, United States Postal Service; bottom, Dan Shulman. 9: NYPL, Picture Collection. 10: top, Culver Pictures; bottom, Courtesy of The Title Guarantee Co. 11: left, LC; right, NYPL. 12: MCNY. 13: top, Larry Bercow; bottom, *1800 Woodcuts by Thomas Bewick and His School*, ed. Blanche Cirker (Dover Publications, Inc., 1962). 14: top, Larry Bercow; bottom, MCNY. 15: center, NYPL, Picture Collection; right, Culver Pictures. 16: MCNY. 17: top, LC; bottom, NYPL, Picture Collection. 18: LC. 19: NYPL, Prints Division, Spencer Collection. 20: LC. 21: Long Island Historical Society. 22-23: NYPL, I.N. Phelps Stokes Collection. 24: left, NYHS; top, NYPL, Picture Collection; bottom, Matthew Lebowitz. 25: top, NYPL; bottom, Anne S.K. Brown Military Collection, Brown University Library. 26: left, MCNY; right, Larry Bercow. 27: left, United States Postal Service; top, LC; bottom, *Picture Source Book for Collage and Decoupage*, ed. Edmund V. Gillon, Jr. (Dover Publications, Inc., 1974). 28: top left, NYPL; top right, National Archives; bottom, NYPL, Picture Collection. 29: MCNY. 30: Ginger Chih. 31: left, Larry Bercow; right, Courtesy of the Martyr's Shrine, Auriesville, New York. 32: MCNY. 33: top, Courtesy of Trinity Church, Wall Street/Coxe-Goldberg Photography, Inc.; bottom, Larry Bercow. 34: left, Courtesy of the Presbyterian Historical Society; top right, Ginger Chih; bottom right, Larry Bercow. 35: top left, NYHS; top right, Larry Bercow; bottom, MCNY. 36: left, NYPL, Picture Collection; right, Larry Bercow. 37: NYPL, Picture Collection. 38: Courtesy of The Chase Manhattan Archives. 40: Larry Bercow. 41: top, NYPL, Picture Collection; right, Ginger Chih. 42: left, NYHS; right, NYPL, Picture Collection. 43: left, LC; right, Berenice Abbott/MCNY. 44: Courtesy of The Title Guarantee Co. 45: Metropolitan Museum of Art, Bequest of Edward W.C. Arnold, 1954. 46: Larry Bercow. 47: NYPL, Picture Collection. 48: NYPL, Picture Collection. 49: NYHS. 50: left, NYHS; right, FDR Library. 51: center, NYHS; bottom, Bettmann Archive; right, Larry Bercow. 52: top, Culver Pictures; bottom, Larry Bercow. 53: left, NYHS; right, NYPL. 54: Brooklyn Museum, Gift of the Atlantic, Gulf and Pacific Co., The Gamble Fund and The Lillian Pitkin Shenk Fund in memory of Charles Debevoise Shenk. 55: Matthew Lebowitz. 56: NYPL. 57: left, NYHS; right, NYPL. 58: NYHS. 59: MCNY. 60: Todd M. Harriman. 61: left, Larry Bercow; top right and bottom, LC. 62: top left and right, NYHS; bottom, Courtesy of St. Luke's-Roosevelt Hospital Center. 63: NYHS. 64: NYHS. 65: NYPL, Schomburg Center. 66: left, NYHS; right, Staten Island Historical Society. 67: MCNY. 68: top, NYHS; bottom, NYPL, Picture Collection. 69: top, Dan Shulman; bottom, Larry Bercow. 70: top, LC; bottom, Larry Bercow. 71: NYHS. 72: left, Courtesy of Independence National Historical Park; right, Larry Bercow. 73: Ginger Chih. 74-75: left, MCNY; right, NYPL, Picture Collection. 76: top left, MCNY, Harry T. Peters Collection; top right, NYHS; bottom, Larry Bercow. 77: left, LC; center, Philadelphia Museum of Art, Given by the New York Life Insurance Co., photography by Will Brown; right, Larry Bercow. 78: NYHS. 79: *The New York News*. 80: left, New York Academy of Medicine; right, Courtesy of Rockefeller Center, Inc. 81: Queensboro Public Library/*New York Herald Tribune* Morgue. 82: NYHS. 83: Compix. 84: left, MCNY; right, Dan Shulman. 85: NYHS. 86: left, LC; right, Frederick Lewis, Inc. 87: New York State Museum. 88: left, Courtesy of The Chase Manhattan Archives; right, LC. 89: left, NYPL; right, Dan Shulman. 90: MCNY. 91: left, NYPL, Picture Collection; right, NYPL, Schomburg Center. 92: top, National Portrait Gallery, Smithsonian Institution, Washington, D.C.; bottom, NYHS. 93: left, Courtesy of the New York Society Library; top right, J.G. Heck, *The Complete Encyclopedia of Illustration*, original edition, 1851; reprinted, 1979, Crown Publishers.; bottom, Courtesy of RCA. 94: Compix. 95: Culver Pictures. 96: NYPL, Picture Collection. 97: top, NYPL, I.N. Phelps Stokes Collection; bottom, NYPL, Picture Collection. 98: left, NYPL, Picture Collection; right, American Philosophical Society. 99: top, NYPL, Picture Collection; bottom, MCNY. 100: LC. 101: LC. 102: left, LC; top right and bottom, NYHS. 103: NYHS. 104: top, LC; bottom, both MCNY. 105: *The New York News*. 106: left, NYPL, Library of the Performing Arts at Lincoln Center, Music Division; right, NYPL, Schomburg Center. 107: top left, LC; top right and bottom, NYHS. 108: left, MCNY; right, Courtesy of Conference House Association, Inc. 109: top, Irwin Glusker; bottom, *The New York News*; right, Wolfgang Hoyt/Esto. 110: left, William Rivelli; right, Robert E. Mates/The Solomon R. Guggenheim Museum. 111: Y. Nagata/United Nations. 112: LC. 113: LC, Rinhart Collection. 114: NYHS. 115: MCNY. 116: NYHS. 117: NYHS. 118: left, NYPL, Picture Collection; center, Courtesy of A.T. & T. Co. Photo Center; right, MCNY. 119: left, MCNY; right, E. Alice Austen/Staten Island Historical Society. 120-121: left, NYPL, Picture Collection; center, Frederic Lewis, Inc.; right, Larry Bercow. 122: top, Courtesy of The Bancroft Library, University of California, Berkeley; bottom, Culver Pictures. 123: Irwin Glusker. 124: top, Courtesy of Rockefeller Center, Inc.; bottom, Library of the New York Botanical Garden, Bronx, New York. 125: Library of the New York Botanical Garden, Bronx, New York. 126: William Rivelli.

The jacket/cover photographs were taken from the following pages in the book: 27, lower right: chiropodist's sign. 49: transvestite governor. 77, center: unclad female statue. 94: Babe Ruth. 102, left: first subway. 121, right: first cocktail.

Acknowledgments

This book could not have been written without the help of a great many people who generously shared their knowledge and resources. I am particularly indebted to Phyllis Barr, archivist/parish recorder of Trinity Church; Victor Tarry, former executive secretary and now honorary secretary of Congregation Shearith Israel; Berthe Schwartz, former secretary for cultural affairs of the Belgian Consulate General in New York; George Salomon of the American Jewish Committee; and Patricia Volk. I am grateful also for the efficient and courteous assistance of the librarians of the local history room of the New York Public Library at 42d Street, of the library's newspaper annex at 43d Street, and of the performing arts branch at Lincoln Center; the librarians of the New York Botanical Garden, the Long Island Historical Society, the American Irish Historical Society, the New-York Historical Society and the Schomburg Center; and Shari Segel of Research Reports.

Henry Moscow